AVID

READER

PRESS

From Mistakes to Meaning

Owning Your Past So It Doesn't Own You

Michael Lynton
and Joshua L. Steiner

AVID READER PRESS

*New York   Amsterdam/Antwerp   London
Toronto   Sydney/Melbourne   New Delhi*

AVID READER PRESS
An Imprint of Simon & Schuster, LLC
1230 Avenue of the Americas
New York, NY 10020

First Avid Reader Press hardcover edition February 2026

AVID READER PRESS and colophon are
trademarks of Simon & Schuster, LLC

Simon & Schuster strongly believes in freedom of expression and stands against censorship in all its forms. For more information, visit BooksBelong.com.

For information about special discounts for bulk purchases, please contact Simon & Schuster Special Sales at 1-866-506-1949 or business@simonandschuster.com.

The Simon & Schuster Speakers Bureau can bring authors to your live event. For more information or to book an event contact the Simon & Schuster Speakers Bureau at 1-866-248-3049 or visit our website at www.simonspeakers.com.

Interior design by Lewelin Polanco

Manufactured in the United States of America

1 3 5 7 9 10 8 6 4 2

Library of Congress Control Number: 2025946226

ISBN 978-1-6680-8022-1
ISBN 978-1-6682-2885-2 (Int Exp)
ISBN 978-1-6680-8024-5 (ebook)

Let's stay in touch! Scan here to get book recommendations, exclusive offers, and more delivered to your inbox.

For Antoinette and Jamie

Contents

PART 1: What Have We Done?

1. It's Time   3

2. Know Thy Schema   19

3. The Velvet Rope   29

4. The Polar Bear   53

PART 2: You're Not Alone

5. The Life Cycle of Mistakes   75

6. The Front Row   81

7. The Lunch Box   85

8. *The Big Year*   105

9. Traffic Stop   129

10. Three's Company   147

11. To *Elle* and Back   159

12. It's Not Having What You Want;
It's Wanting What You Have   171

Contents

13. Portrait of an Artist as a Young Man   185

14. If You Break It, You Own It   197

15. Running Man   209

PART 3: Onward Through Openness

16. How to Talk About Mistakes   223

17. How to Make Fewer Mistakes   231

18. The Water Is Lovely   241

Acknowledgments   245

Notes   249

PART 1

What
Have
We
Done?

1

It's Time

L ate one night in 2015, Michael called Josh in a panic. Months earlier, the North Korean government had hacked Sony Entertainment, shutting down its operations and leaking company secrets. As CEO, Michael had been spending twenty-hour days reassuring colleagues, answering questions from the Tokyo headquarters, and trying to get help from the FBI as he managed one of the worst corporate IT crises in history.

WikiLeaks had taken thousands of Sony documents, posted them online, and created a search function that allowed reporters to find the gossip that Sony executives had unwisely committed to writing. Story after story appeared about salaries, movie budgets, and casting decisions, along with deeply troubling comments about race and gender.

Through the WikiLeaks search function, reporters discovered that Michael had used his corporate email for personal matters as well. Suddenly, the crisis became intimate; the world could find sensitive information about Michael's family—including his children. Having spent so much of his energy and political capital trying to protect his colleagues, he now worried about his three daughters.

On that late-night call, as Michael explained the risk, Josh appreciated why Michael sounded so agitated, angry, and eager for help. Michael was at his best, totally focused on his family, and at his worst, almost incoherent with rage and fear. Unknown to Josh, but very much on Michael's mind, was that he had personally green-lit the movie, *The Interview*, that had enraged the North Koreans. That one decision, that terrible mistake, had upended thousands of lives.

Michael blasted his emotions at Josh in a long rant. By the end of the call, we had devised a plan that ameliorated some of Michael's anxiety. The call—painful, confusing, and frustrating—actually made us closer. Michael revealed aspects of himself that might have taken years to come out under normal circumstances.

That was the last meaningful conversation we had about the hack for more than five years. The door slammed shut on one of the most traumatic episodes of Michael's life. For five years, whenever Josh asked about the impact of the hack on Michael's emotions or his outlook on the world, Michael changed the subject. Sometimes, as we often do with each other, he used humor to deflect. Other times, he would testily make clear that he did not want to discuss it. No one, not his family, colleagues, or friends, got another glance.

Michael's reticence annoyed Josh in the way that we all get upset by seeing our own shortcomings manifested in others. For years before the hack, we had almost exactly opposite roles: Michael as inquisitor, Josh as the artful dodger. Michael nudged, prodded, and practically begged Josh to talk about how his private diary had become damning evidence in the Clinton Whitewater scandal. As chief of staff at the Treasury Department, Josh had become front-page news as part of the investigation that ultimately led to the revelation of President Clinton's affair with Monica Lewinsky and his impeachment trial.

As with Michael and the hack, Josh refused to talk about his experience. At the slightest mention of the word *diary*, he would laugh nervously and push the subject aside.

We had each made incredibly painful mistakes that, despite a decades-long friendship, we refused to discuss—with each other or anyone else.

We talked about everything else. When Michael got prostate cancer, Josh heard about all the unappealing side effects. When Josh's rigidity and perfectionism damaged family vacations, Michael got the details. Bad parenting? We know what each other's children have endured. Marriage? We share how our respective long-suffering wives call out our regular missteps. We've celebrated and mourned together, and traveled and enjoyed endless dinners in each other's company.

We've left virtually no historical or emotional stone unturned. Except for our biggest mistakes. They weren't secrets. Indeed, both had generated headlines, but we had hidden them in plain sight beneath deep layers of shame and anger. Mistakes that had altered our careers, changed our views of ourselves and the world, and stayed with us long after the rest of the world moved on. Two people who had every possible advantage growing up—loving and demanding parents, supportive siblings, "prestigious" educations—had never had the courage to talk about their worst moments.

Until one day during COVID, when we took a beach walk along the Atlantic. Maybe we had run out of British police procedurals to discuss. Maybe we felt worn down by the pandemic. Or perhaps the threat of death or serious illness made us realize that the window for telling the truth might close without warning.

Almost certainly, our age had an impact on our decision. Erik Erikson famously wrote about the eight stages of psychosocial development, which culminate in "integrity versus despair."[1] Unsurprisingly, we wanted to believe that we had made progress on "integrity" by leading fulfilling, purposeful lives. We also knew, however, that we felt some bitterness and regret that risked metastasizing into "despair." We hoped that by coming clean about what hadn't gone well we could mitigate that risk and might even increase our sense of purpose. For all those reasons, for the first time we decided to talk about our mistakes.

Our efforts began slowly and rather unsuccessfully. You can't go from hiding to open confessional overnight. For someone just learning how to swim, the high dive looks scary. So, we talked about relatively trivial mistakes: the time that Michael blew up at a friend for being late; and when Josh left the speech for a presidential candidate on the campaign plane. We moved on to more significant ones when we had said things that hurt people we loved or let ambition swamp judgment.

When we finally got around to the Sony hack and Josh's diary, we recounted facts and chronologies rather than reactions and feelings. We skimmed over the parts that had caused the deep wounds and dwelled on the anecdotes that didn't reveal our underlying emotions.

We had to encourage and prod each other; it took attempt after attempt. We learned to trust each other—to trust our reactions and questions, and respect our fears and embarrassment. Importantly, we provided each other with positive reinforcement that allowed even greater honesty. The honesty provided relief.

As we unpacked our ugly mistakes and pushed each other to unveil the truth, we became more and more intrigued about what we learned. We began to wonder what would happen if we gave our mistakes the kind of empathetic, open treatment that we use for our most serious conversations about relationships or work. We wondered if that process might make mistakes windows into parts of our lives that we had previously hidden. We hoped that opening that window would help us relate better to our families and friends, operate more effectively at work, and feel better about ourselves.

We came to believe that mistakes reveal hidden aspects of our histories and personalities. If that was true for us, we thought others might feel similarly. We asked our spouses and friends about the topic. They too had buried mistakes.

Then we expanded the circle even further to some of the most interesting, intelligent people we knew—inside our families and out. Normally, when you call someone accomplished and request an interview, you ask about their greatest successes. We did the opposite.

We asked people to tell us about a mistake that they deeply regretted. In some cases, we knew about a mistake that we thought that they had never discussed. With others, we simply asked if they had a story, like ours, that they had never examined.

The more we learned, the more we wanted to know, so we began to look for articles and books about mistakes. There simply aren't a lot. While excellent books covered aspects of our questions, we couldn't find one that gave us the framework we needed to understand what had happened or why. Nothing we read made us feel like part of a broader community of people who had also made mistakes. Nothing gave us permission to talk about something that had for years felt so pathetic.

We had gone from refusing to talk about our mistakes, to becoming intensely curious about them, to being frustrated that we couldn't get the answers we needed. That's when we decided to write this book. We quickly realized that we needed an expert guide.

Happily, we met Dr. Alison Papadakis, a teaching professor at Johns Hopkins University who became our key partner. Alison, who's a clinical psychologist, helped us find the academic evidence to support our hypotheses and, equally important, let us know in no uncertain terms when our ideas were bunk. She brought just the right combination of academic expertise and practical experience.

She helped us think about how what happens before a mistake can lead to poor decisions—and the healthy and unhealthy ways people process the regret that follows. She served as our guide in that dark region known as the human psyche. We could not have found a better fellow explorer.

Through our reflections, interviews, and research, we've come to believe that mistakes don't get the attention they deserve. For years, we thought that they "just happen"—like rain on a wedding day: unfortunate, but out of our control. What's the point of examining something that's unavoidable?

It turns out that they don't just happen. They follow patterns and have identifiable causes. Instead of treating them like unlucky accidents, we want to talk about them as openly as we do our major life events. They're a bit like broken bones: if they don't get properly reset, the aftermath becomes far worse than the accident itself. By discussing and analyzing our mistakes and those of the other people you'll read about in this book, we believe that we can all transform how we feel about ourselves, our family, friends, and colleagues.

This is a storybook, but it's not a "hero's journey"—one mistake after another doesn't lead to a magical outcome. But by treating the mistakes seriously, and telling and retelling these stories, by unpacking them like Russian nesting dolls and then lining up all the dolls in order, we formed narratives. They became less mysterious, more comprehensible, and eventually, as a result, they lost their power over us.

In the first chapters of this book, we describe our two mistakes in all their unseemly glory. How Michael made a rash decision that caused one of the worst corporate breaches in American history. How Josh kept an ill-advised diary that embarrassed the White House and landed him on the front page of *The New York Times*. Then you'll read about the mistakes of people who generously told us about their own terrible moments.

As you will read in later chapters, Malcolm Gladwell, the author, described a passion that he abandoned; Karol Mason, the president of John Jay College of Criminal Justice, recounted a painful interaction with the police; Michael Govan, director of the Los Angeles County Museum of Art, reflected on a career choice that he regretted; Irv Gotti, the music impresario, lamented a terrible interview that destroyed a friendship.

They, and many others, took the plunge right alongside us. During the interviews, we witnessed tears and shame; we also sensed catharsis. Once we started, we never had to turn back. Each mistake felt fully worthy of exploration.

As they say on *Law & Order*, these are their stories—raw and often full of regret. They form the backbone of this book. They are not hypothetical or imaginary, but real chronicles of painful human experience. In their individuality, they illuminate larger, more universal phenomena that apply to all of us at one time or another.

To analyze those phenomena, we needed definitions that captured what we had experienced and gave us insights into what we had felt. When we couldn't find just what we wanted, we considered bank shots: mistakes and failures seem like synonyms, and we knew that failure has received lots of attention. So, we began to study failure.

Historians love ambitious failures. Would we remember the Battle of Thermopylae as vividly if the Greeks had won? Ernest Shackleton's expedition never crossed Antarctica, and it nearly killed his crew, but the *Endurance* lives on in our imagination. The Apollo 13 mission stays imprinted in our memory precisely because it failed.

That's unsurprising since these stories inspire us by virtue of their heroism and perseverance. Failure led to success of a very different kind: the celebration of the human capacity for teamwork and survival. It's true in business too. The *Harvard Business Review* devoted an entire issue to failure.

We think failures usually follow a similar pattern: painstaking planning that includes careful risk assessments, a series of important accomplishments along the way, and then an unsuccessful outcome. To fail, one must have strived to fulfill a real achievement—usually with the help of others. Failure requires a level of self-awareness about the ultimate goal coupled with a determined resolve to reach it.

Those characteristics are actually quite similar to success—except the outcome. We remember and applaud both Neil Armstrong and Shackleton. One landed on the moon; the other failed to cross the Antarctic continent. Both relied on years of preparation by legions of people in service of reaching a seemingly impossible destination. We draw inspiration from both despite their very different conclusions.

Failure isn't just the opposite of success; it's actually a sibling. Success and failure come after planning, commitment, and hard work in pursuit of an ambitious goal.

Those attributes make success and failure worthy of study, which is why you can find so many books about them. But our mistakes involved something very different. As you will read, we had made decisions without consulting with or listening to other people. We had acted on impulse, emotion, or old habits. Our actions did not come close to qualifying as noble failures.

Mistakes can feel as if they can come out of nowhere. We've all been there. We stub our toe on a corner, kick the wall in anger, and end up hobbling around with a broken bone. Then, when people ask us how we hurt ourselves, we either blame a poorly located wall or pretend that our toe doesn't hurt. When they point out that we're limping, we claim that it's just a blister. We're so embarrassed and angry that we lie. And, if anyone points out that we have a pattern of turning small hiccups into major mistakes, we practically boil over. A small accident, stubbing our toe, turns into a mistake when we decide to kick the wall and then lie about it.

At work, we get overcommitted, forget to read materials before a meeting, and then get teased when we ask a question that got answered in what we had failed to read. We then react defensively and get the reputation as someone who's thin-skinned.

When we make these kinds of impulsive mistakes, we may not even know that we're making an important decision or any decision at all. There is rarely anything thoughtful about the process, and the result often leaves us feeling embarrassed.

As you'll see from the stories in the book, many much more serious mistakes have remarkably similar characteristics to the kinds we make in our daily lives.

Here's our definition of a mistake: a decision taken without careful consideration or self-awareness that causes regret. Compare that to a failure, which follows hard work and planning and often leads to learning and growth.

There's no bright line where one begins and another ends, but try thinking of it this way:

Great mountain climbers make meticulous plans to achieve an incredibly difficult goal and still sometimes don't reach the summit. They "fail" to reach their goal. The same climber might forget to call home to let her family know that she got safely back to base camp. That's a "mistake" that stresses out the people she loves.

At its simplest: marriages "fail." Drunken Vegas weddings are generally "mistakes." In the case of marriage, two people come together in the hope of living meaningful lives as a couple—until death do them part; they have an ambitious goal, and, sometimes, they fail to achieve it. Marrying someone you meet after four cocktails doesn't take a lot of planning, and the goal is usually not entirely obvious. No wonder we hide that kind of mistake: no one wants to get ridiculed for such bad judgment.

Now, if you get married after four cocktails or kick a door in anger, is that really a decision? Our answer is yes. A bad one, but still a decision. We believe that even impulsive actions constitute decisions. No one forced you to kick the door or get married. Sure, you made it without careful consideration (Vegas wedding) or self-awareness (you get so angry that you kick the door), but that's what makes it a mistake. And, if you make a decision that rolls out over years, that too can constitute a mistake even if it didn't occur in one defining moment.

With that definition in hand, we began to think of all the different types of mistakes. Once you get started, it's hard to stop: you overreact, procrastinate, brag, rush to judgment, lie, catastrophize, drink too much, show bias, and become impulsive. That's before you become impatient, distracted, self-absorbed, intolerant, and venal.

We started to drown in all of the ways we make bad decisions. There were so many of such different types that we couldn't find any organizing principles. We weren't the first to try.

For literally thousands of years, people have tried to classify mistakes. They've used categories to try to improve behavior and enforce religious orthodoxy. Aristotle's *Rhetoric* classified virtues and vices: "All the actions of men must necessarily be referred to seven causes: chance, nature, compulsion, habit, reason, anger, and desire."[2]

Platonic thought broke a person down into the body, the soul, and the mind, and then early Egyptian Christians assigned a series of problems that went along with each of them. The body had nutritional and sexual needs. The soul could make people argumentative or rude. And the mind could lead one to envy and hubris.

Eastern religions give us further classifications. Buddhism warns that we will encounter five hindrances while trying to achieve enlightenment and nirvana: sensory desire, aversion, sloth and torpor, restlessness and remorse, and doubt.[3]

In Judaism, you find three types of sin: *pesha* (deliberate sin, committed in defiance), *avon* (lust, perversity), and *chet* (unintentional sin, human fault).[4]

By the sixth century, Pope Gregory I codified what we now call the seven deadly sins: pride, greed, lust, envy, gluttony, wrath, and sloth.

Almost all the historical efforts came with a healthy dollop of judgment. As Kathryn Schulz writes in *Being Wrong*, many people think that "our errors are evidence of our gravest social, intellectual, and moral failings." For centuries, "in our collective imagination, error is associated not just with shame and stupidity but also with ignorance, indolence, psychopathology, and moral degeneracy."[5]

We don't think of ourselves as degenerates and certainly didn't come to view the people we interviewed as indolent or stupid. Religious and moral language just didn't fit the stories that we heard or how we felt about ourselves.

We'd done something wrong, but ethics and religion alone hadn't given us the way to figure it out. Perhaps we could find the answer in academia.

In fields such as medicine and aircraft maintenance, there are psychological studies and technical literature on why we make professional mistakes and keep them hidden. To help in those jobs, where mistakes can prove so costly, scholars have devised precise classifications.

James Reason, professor of psychology at the University of Manchester and a world-leading expert in human errors, has written thoughtfully about the differences between errors, slips, lapses, and mistakes. The research demonstrates the complexity of classifying and understanding even relatively straightforward mistakes.

Imagine an airplane pilot flips the wrong switch. Reason refers to that broad category of problem as an "error." In Reason's language, that is "a planned sequence of mental or physical activities [that] fails to achieve its intended outcome [and is not due to] some chance agency."[6]

Put differently, turbulence didn't push the pilot's hand onto the wrong switch. So, what else could have caused it? Maybe the switch had poor labeling (that's a "slip," an action that did not go as planned) or the pilot forgot a step in the correct sequence (a "lapse," an error due to a memory glitch). Or, if the person who wrote the checklist had organized it poorly or not made clear its intended purpose, that's closer to a "mistake," an error in the plan.

Reason's work and that of others in the related field of cognition helped us understand specialized problems. Appropriately, the academic research has precise and somewhat esoteric descriptions relating to problems with regularly repeated, mission-critical tasks, but that didn't get us much closer to the kind of experiences we had had. The mistakes that interested us didn't involve those kinds of sequences or processes. Ours involved fluid situations in which emotions and other people's actions played crucial roles.

We felt a little like detectives before the development of professional policing techniques. For most of history, society focused on the crime: Who did what to whom? Authorities tortured suspects and made assumptions based on stereotypes, but did not employ a systematic approach to understanding why the crime occurred. In the nineteenth century, Hans Gross, an Austrian jurist and criminologist, articulated and popularized the now widely adopted investigative technique of considering "motive, opportunity, and means." He set out a crucial three-part process that worked with almost all cases. Prior to Gross's systematic approach, criminal investigations relied on the intuition and subjective interpretations of the investigators.[7]

We too needed to stop relying on "intuition and . . . subjective interpretations." Examining failures hadn't helped. Morality, ethics, and religion made us feel guilty, and didn't even get us closer to figuring out why we had made the mistakes or how to get over our shame. We knew that we hadn't committed crimes, but we thought about our mistakes in the same way that police acted before Gross formalized his approach: we tortured ourselves and applied all sorts of assumptions and judgments.

Even if we hadn't committed any crimes, Gross's recognition of the importance of "motive" gave us an important clue. We realized that while a mistake can take place in an instant, what happens before the mistake makes just as big a difference. All our initial lists of mistakes failed to capture cause and effect—the way our pasts influence our behavior and affect how we process what we've done.

In *A Swim in the Pond in the Rain*, George Saunders, the remarkable author and teacher, writes, "Causality is to the writer what melody is to the songwriter: a superpower that the audience feels as the crux of the matter; the thing the audience actually shows up for."[8]

What Saunders recommends for writers echoes what we all learn as children: cause and effect. Break the rules: get punished. Do well: get a reward. Drop a glass: watch it break. Saunders knows that it drives good writing. We all know that it drives a lot of life.

We get angry and shout hurtful words; we grow impatient and cancel worthwhile plans; we cut corners and hurt our reputations; we gossip and alienate our friends. It's easy to come up with another one hundred examples.

As we thought about those examples of "cause and effect," we realized that the kinds of mistakes that interested us the most related to emotions and behavioral patterns. We had spent so much of our lives reasoning our way through problems and had still made these terrible mistakes. Our "thinking" had only taken us so far. We hadn't given sufficient weight to our emotions or figured out how to tell stories about ourselves.

To understand "cause," what happens before the decision, and "effect," how we process our regret, we needed to understand how our mistakes fit into the larger continua of our lives. We had begun our explorations thinking of mistakes as events that take place in a moment—the instant when you make a bad decision—but we realized that just the way motive provokes the crime, mistakes actually take place over a longer time. There's your life before the mistake. There's what's happening during the moment you make the decision. Then there's what happens after it. To figure out what happened and, more important, why, you have to go back and forth in time.

There is no shortage of ways to think about that time sequence: before, during, after. Or, backstory, action, and consequences. Whether for pleasure or work, we all use stories to convey ideas. From the Bible to *The Iliad* to the origin stories of successful companies, narratives help us absorb ethics and ideas.

Syd Field, in his famous book on screenwriting,[9] universalized this storytelling process and gave it three parts: the setup, confrontation, and resolution. You need all three to define a story: a confrontation on its own has no interest. The audience wants to understand what caused it and how it gets resolved. Our lives follow a somewhat similar pattern. From Greek mythology, it's the riddle of the Sphinx: What starts on four legs, goes to two, and ends up with three? Humans. We crawl, walk, and then use a cane. The three acts of our lives.

Only after we unpacked our mistakes did we realize that they almost always took place over an extended time. Even if the frame gets frozen at the very moment of action, rarely does any event that matters occur in isolation.

Remember the definition of a mistake: a decision taken without careful consideration or self-awareness that causes regret. To really understand that mistake, you need to divide it into three parts. What happened before you made that decision? What was going on that prevented you from careful consideration or having self-awareness? And then how did you handle your regret?

This book will argue that our most important mistakes almost invariably follow a three-act structure. Act I: what happened BEFORE the decision. Act II: what's happening DURING the time you make the decision. Act III: how you handle the regret AFTER your decision.

When people told us their stories, they started the conversation thinking that they had identified "the" mistake: their bad decision. They all started their stories in Act II. That's understandable. If you tell the story of slamming the door on your colleague, you don't usually start by explaining all the bad things that had happened in your day before the argument. Nor do you begin with saying how badly you feel about it.

As we discussed our mistakes and those of the people we interviewed, our views evolved; we came to believe that when it comes to serious mistakes, there are no one-act plays. Each serious mistake involves a bad decision, but what happens before and after can prove even more important.

That's because mistakes fall within the arc of our lives. We experience every event through the prism of what preceded it. Even on our most ordinary days we confront so many stimuli that we need a way to process them without having to figure them out afresh each time. We use previous examples that help us make sense of what we're seeing, and we consolidate those experiences into mental models.

How, we wondered, does that history shape our perceptions, emotions, and reactions in ways that can lead to mistakes?

2

Know Thy Schema

I n 1981, psychologists William Brewer and James Treyens performed an experiment that showed how much our pasts shape our perceptions. They told their volunteers that before the experiment "began," they had to wait in an office while someone else finished. After a brief stop in the office, the volunteers took a memory test of what they saw inside it. The subjects hadn't realized that the experiment was actually a test of what they remembered.[1]

The volunteers were much more likely to remember things that they thought belonged in an office than the objects that didn't belong in a typical one. And they remembered objects such as books that weren't even in the office. They had a visual "template" for how an office should appear that overrode what they actually saw. The template came from the volunteers' memories and experiences of seeing many different offices. Through those experiences, they developed and remembered a prototypical office, which they applied to the real world. As Henry David Thoreau wrote, "The question is not what you look at, but what you see."[2]

Those templates work well with "thinking" problems—how does an office look, where do I pay at a grocery store. Life, however, brings a more complex set of experiences in which we need a broader way to interpret what we face. The technical term for that broader "template"— the combination of all those memories and experiences—is "schema,"[3] a concept developed by the Swiss psychologist Jean Piaget.[4]

Schemas serve two important purposes. First, they shape our perceptions based on how we've previously interacted with the world. They are abstractions that help us interpret what we see. Second, they influence how we react based on our perceptions of what we're seeing. Schemas help us both make sense of what we see and select how to react to it.

Consider a relative who gets annoyed at family gatherings when asked to do even a trivial chore. He overreacts in a way that clearly feels like a mistake and then slinks off into a corner. Probably, his initial reaction—getting angry at the request—had little to do with the request and a lot to do with what had happened in the past. Maybe he feels that since childhood he consistently got assigned a disproportionately large share of the family chores. His decision to storm off reflects all the anger of past events. Those past events, consolidated in his schema, influence his perception of the situation. You see him getting asked to do one small task; he sees a pattern of unfairness.

We develop our schemas in childhood and continually revise them with new experiences throughout our lives. Sometimes we adapt through conscious effort. In other instances, we simply adapt through experience. Dr. Aaron Beck, a professor of psychiatry at the University of Pennsylvania who developed cognitive behavioral therapy (CBT) and did much of the foundational research on how schemas shape emotional and behavioral responses, described schemas as the structures we use to store information about our self-perception, views of others, goals, expectations, and memories.[5]

Two examples:

After dating for three years, Josh's then girlfriend and now wife, Antoinette, gave Josh a choice: get married or break up. Josh wrote long lists about whether they should or should not get married. They included all her virtues and all their cultural and religious differences.

What Josh didn't do was recognize that his list reflected his schema about marriage. For years he'd carried around a mental image of the "right" person for him. Antoinette checked none of the boxes on religion or background, which made him obsess about those without even realizing why.

Antoinette understandably grew impatient. The two almost broke up. Instead, they went to a therapist, who helped them talk about their dynamics and the schemas they each brought to the relationship. Through discussion, Josh identified his schema about the "right" person and learned to trust his emotions. If only Selena Gomez had come along a little sooner singing "The Heart Wants What It Wants." By not understanding his schema, Josh almost made the biggest possible mistake—losing Antoinette.

Our schemas interfere with our day-to-day lives as well. When someone keeps Michael waiting at a restaurant, he can quickly get annoyed. Why is that his instinct? It's at least partly because, as a child, Michael's parents insisted on punctuality. They taught him that being late meant that you didn't value the time of the person whom you kept waiting. His schema associates being kept waiting with being disrespected.

His schema also shapes his reaction. While he knows that uncontrollable factors might come into play (e.g., traffic), he gets annoyed. That's understandable—no one likes to feel disrespected. Importantly, in his childhood, he saw his father get annoyed when people kept him waiting. Now, Michael takes punctuality seriously.

Compare Michael's schema about punctuality with someone whose schema makes him believe that he is unlikable and always wrong. If that person is kept waiting, he might wonder if he'd done something to offend his guest, or whether he'd mistaken the time and location. An anxious person's schema would drive them to a very different conclusion from Michael's based on the same situation. That might lead to a different mistake: becoming overly apologetic to the point of appearing deeply insecure or avoiding social events altogether.

It's unrealistic to think that Michael will ever stop trying to be on time, but knowing the source of his annoyance makes him less likely to get snarky when someone keeps him waiting; knowledge allows him to remember that his schema sometimes activates a disproportionate reaction. The impatience doesn't disappear; his self-knowledge helps mitigate the impact by considering that factors other than rudeness might account for the delay.

Our schemas can be as narrow as how an office should look or as broad as how we relate to our peers. They get formed early and influence so many of our interactions. How they influence us may change based on our moods and external forces, and they get modified by new experiences, but they never disappear.

It's important to remember that while we form some of our most powerful schemas as children, they continue to evolve as we age. In some cases, we develop completely new ones based on the experiences we have as teenagers and adults. Put differently, yes, at times it's all about your childhood, but that's only the first stop on the journey. It brings to mind that old expression, "Past experience should be a guidepost, not a hitching post."

Your schemas can only serve you well if you understand the situation you face. A healthy, useful schema that gets misapplied doesn't provide the insight that's needed. What works in one context will lead to bad mistakes in another.

There's a television advertisement in which a guy shows up for a "fantasy" football party dressed as a centaur. Wrong kind of fantasy. An embarrassing mistake that leaves him ashamed by his friends' reactions. Just as ignorance of the law is no defense (you'll still get a ticket even if you didn't see the speed limit sign), not knowing about the situation won't make it any less embarrassing.

That's why it's so important to know where you are. In a much more elegant way, that's the question David Foster Wallace asked when addressing the Kenyon College 2005 graduation:

> There are these two young fish swimming along and they happen to meet an older fish swimming the other way, who nods at them and says, "Morning, boys. How's the water?"
>
> And the two young fish swim on for a bit, and then eventually one of them looks over at the other and goes, "What the hell is water?"[6]

The metaphor applies to many of us. We become so habituated to our environment that we stop noticing it. In other cases, the work at hand—for a fish, that's swimming—doesn't allow us to pay close attention to our context. Forward motion keeps us engaged and productive but doesn't allow much time or energy to reflect on how we need to adjust to our environments.

When students first get to college, they benefit from staying up late talking with their friends about the world. There's such sensory overload—new people, new classes, living away from home—that students need ways to process what they experience. When they graduate and get their first job, they have a whole new set of stimuli. But if they stay up late every night talking with their roommates, the job probably won't last. What works in one stage of life can be a bad mistake in another. Our schemas and old habits from previous experiences don't always work in new contexts.

So many of our daily interactions rely on the schemas we develop over a lifetime—the ways we interact with baristas, colleagues, and friends would all become exhausting if we didn't have some instinctive sense of how to respond to "How was your weekend?" or "Do you have time to take a quick look at this project?" By developing socially acceptable responses, we avoid having every experience, and therefore every response, feel brand-new. Every time you negotiate with friends over where to go to dinner or you ask for a raise, you're using your schemas to understand how others might react. You can study them and become familiar with them, but you can't outrun them.

When they work well, schemas help us function effectively and regulate our emotions. When they're applied rigidly or are negatively biased, they can lead to mental health challenges and poor decision-making.[7]

If you don't know your schemas, it's hard to know why you react the way you do. As you'll read in Michael's story, the schemas he developed in his childhood had a profound impact on how he interacted with his colleagues when he made his mistake. Understanding what happened before he made his decision is essential to understanding why he made his mistake.

When Michael was growing up, his mother liked to quote an old German expression that he didn't really understand: "You can't jump over your own shadow." As a child, Michael knew what it meant physically after having tried unsuccessfully to do it. Not until we started reading about schemas, however, did the expression make sense. Your shadow follows you everywhere and changes the complexion of everything it crosses. That shadow is like one of your schemas. It may vary based on the angle of the sun, but its shape always relates to you and it never disappears.

Recognizing your schemas reduces the risk that it feels as if the world is happening to you. Carl Jung said, "The psychological rule says that when an inner situation is not made conscious, it happens outside, as fate."[8]

None of this is easy: neither identifying your schemas nor remembering how they shape perceptions. It's equally hard to process what happens after your mistake. Alas, we both tried to forget all about ours and discouraged anyone from asking about them.

We were like athletes who cover their faces with their hands after dropping a ball or missing a goal. We wanted to hide. But like the images we've all seen on television during those blown plays, the attempt to hide only makes the mistake more obvious while simultaneously making it harder to focus on the next play.

Before our walk on the beach, we had tried to suppress our memories, and that only made the shame grow and mutate. In 1863, Fyodor Dostoevsky wrote, "Try to pose for yourself this task: not to think of a polar bear, and you will see that the cursed thing will come to mind every minute." Struck by Dostoevsky's point, Harvard professor Daniel Wegner conducted the "white bear study" in the 1980s.[9]

He asked one group of participants to suppress thinking about a white bear. When he then asked the group to think about the bear, they thought about it more frequently than a group who were only asked to think about the bear without suppressing it first. As it turns out, Dostoevsky was right: the more you try not to think about something, the more it pops into your mind.

Diana Cioffi and James Holloway further supported the hypothesis, using physical pain to illustrate the point. In their experiments, subjects held an uncomfortably cold object and were given three separate sets of instructions: think about their home, focus on the sensation in their hand, or suppress the sensation in their hand.

The two researchers then assessed the pain two minutes after removing the cold object. Those who monitored the pain recovered the fastest, and those who suppressed it the slowest.[10] We've come to appreciate from Wegner's research that "the suppression of thoughts acts to hide skeletons in the closet and so to provide for later capricious scarings."[11]

It turns out that while embarrassment, guilt, shame, and anxiety all cause discomfort, by refusing to talk about the hack and the diary, we made it worse. We know that partly because of research on one of the most effective treatment techniques for anxiety and trauma: exposure therapy. For over one hundred years, mental health professionals have recognized that providing patients with gradual exposure to their phobias reduces their sensitivity and allows them to lessen their fears. Certain stimuli trigger the flood of memories that cause discomfort.

Exposure to those stimuli reduces their power and helps lower the pain of the underlying event. As Ralph Waldo Emerson reportedly said, "Do the thing we fear, and death of fear is certain." We didn't appreciate the power of that approach until we started writing this book. Once we understood the dangers of suppression and learned that many people fall into our same trap, it made it easier to change and to forgive ourselves. We realized that if doctors can find ways to talk about their mistakes that cost lives, we can find ways to talk openly about what happened and ultimately judge ourselves less harshly.

By embracing regret, we began to "see" our mistakes differently— as events that can signify important aspects of personalities and backgrounds, but don't have to define us. They had power and impact, yet did not need to be mysterious. Demystifying them does not mean minimizing their importance, just as writing about them doesn't make them overly significant. Owning our pasts lessened their power over us.

This book is an invitation into the gnarly complexity of mistakes. An invitation to consider the ways mistakes reflect and shape our relationships, careers, and personalities. It's an invitation to destigmatize mistakes by talking about them.

We hope this book will help you tell someone you trust the story of a mistake you have made. We think that creating a structured narrative around the mistake—an honest recounting, not a novel—will help you to describe what happened before, during, and after you made a decision that you regret. Narratives not only help us find meaning, but also let us identify the patterns that emerge over and over. This can help you avoid repeating them.

Just as we've decided to reveal something that caused us deep shame, and just as the people we interviewed so generously allowed us to tell their stories, maybe you'll do the same. Think of this as an opportunity to reopen cold cases. To see if they lose their power when exposed to your honest and open analysis.

There's that old adage "Learn from your mistakes!" Don't touch a hot stove twice. We have a different kind of learning in mind. We think that your mistakes reveal more about yourself than even your greatest triumphs or most painful failures. Telling the stories of mistakes forced us, in some ways for the first time, to confront our schemas and understand how they shaped our behavior.

While "bad things come in threes," mistakes often ambush you at moments when life feels quite good. That's what happened to Michael.

3

The Velvet Rope

M ichael tells the story himself. At 8:30 a.m. on November 24, 2014, I drove my white Volkswagen GTI out of Brentwood toward Culver City, home of Sony Pictures. The sun glistened off the windows, the immaculate lawns and gorgeous cars filled my view, the joggers in their matching sets and sun visors made me smile. A typical morning in Los Angeles.

My thoughts turned to Sony's weekly marketing meeting. In recent months, the meetings had depressed me: the underwhelming film slate meant long, awkward silences and the real risk of throwing good money after bad. But this Christmas season, Sony had *Annie*, which looked like a winner following other successes such as *The Equalizer* and *21 Jump Street*. As CEO, I felt a combination of optimism and relief.

Just as I turned onto Bundy Drive, the location of an enormous billboard for *The Penguins of Madagascar*, my phone rang. The exact spot stays firmly etched in my memory.

David Hendler, Sony's CFO, didn't even say hello. "Michael, we appear to have a major problem with our IT systems. All of our email systems are down. But what is stranger is that many of our computers seem to be malfunctioning as well."

"Malfunctioning. What do you mean?"

Hendler practically shouted, "I mean they're fried. We can't get them to work at all. I am hearing about it from all over the studio."

I could do nothing other than listen. And drive a little faster toward work.

Sony Studios sat on the old MGM lot. *Gone with the Wind* was shot there, and from the outside it looked as if not much had changed: forty-four acres of soundstages, art deco buildings dating back to the 1930s, and a fake old-fashioned Main Street with building facades meant to look like storefronts. The same man who designed the Oscar statuette, Cedric Gibbons, had designed the Thalberg Building, where I had my office. At the gate to the studio stood a newly installed sculpture, an enormous metal rainbow, 140 feet at its apex, reminding visiting tourists that *The Wizard of Oz* was filmed here as well. The place exuded happiness and fantasy—the polar opposite of what waited for me at work that day.

By the time I walked up the stairs of the Thalberg Building, I began to sense that Sony had a very big problem. Unable to access their emails or any of Sony's systems, the employees had begun to mill around in front of the offices. I spotted Steve Bernard, the head of security, who knew no more than Hendler's worrying report. Nothing worked.

Studios, even large ones such as Sony with its fifteen thousand employees, operate like college campuses, with lots of buildings housing small teams who work independently. On normal days, that work stays hidden inside enormous soundstages and cramped writing rooms. That day, as I walked toward Hendler's office, passing the Jimmy Stewart Theater and Judy Garland Building, dozens and dozens of confused and nervous people had streamed out on the streets. In the canteen, executives, grips, and electricians, who all got to work early, shared anxious gossip.

I found Hendler and Sony's head of IT: grown men, experts in their fields, veterans of endless digital battles. Guys who did not get flustered. Ever. Except now. They both looked scared and confused. Not only could they not access their systems, the head of IT reported that 70 percent of the Sony servers were irreparably damaged. Sony could not make, edit, or release movies, use its email, or access its financial records or production systems. They didn't know what, if anything, the hackers had stolen before the system crashed. They just knew that we didn't have any system at all.

It was one of the worst hacks in corporate history. The entire company ground to a halt. And then over the next few days and weeks it only got worse: the hackers released stolen emails that revealed terrible judgment, confidential scripts, and personal information—including my family's.

Almost immediately the FBI opened an investigation, and evidence suggested that the North Korean government likely led this attack as retribution. It was a surreal moment when it dawned on me that a sovereign nation with nuclear capability, North Korea, would seek to destroy an American company. Why? Simply to quash the release of a film called *The Interview*, a Seth Rogen comedy about a bunch of journalists who make a screwball plan to assassinate the leader of North Korea, Kim Jong Un.

Eight months later, after it became clear that the North Koreans had hacked Sony, after the studio had lost its relationships with many of its most important stars—including Will Smith, Adam Sandler, and Angelina Jolie—I spoke to President Obama about the whole incident. Unsurprisingly, he asked the right question: "What were you thinking when you made killing the leader of a hostile foreign nation a plot point? Of course that was a mistake."

The mistake: my decision to green-light *The Interview*. A decision I made on the fly, outside my usual process.

To understand why I made that decision, you have to go back in time.

Growing up in Holland, I watched a lot of Hollywood movies while perched on the folding chairs of a tiny theater in the small village of Wassenaar. All of the movies captivated me: good, bad, American, European. *The Sting* and *Logan's Run* held equal sway. From cold, dark, frugal Holland, Hollywood seemed magical and totally aspirational: a fantasy, an imaginary place six thousand miles away.

Yet there I was in Hollywood, forty years later, attending a table read of *The Interview*, a new movie starring Seth Rogen and James Franco. The plot of the movie involved two hapless television journalists recruited by the US government to assassinate Kim Jong Un. Despite having run Sony for more than ten years, I still felt excited—partly because I hadn't lost my sense of wonder. That wonder, however, often felt tempered because I spent a lot more time on budgets, benefits plans, and advertising campaigns than working on actual movies.

Walking into the room, I immediately felt energized and simultaneously completely out of place. Although middle-aged, I had not lost the observational skills I'd learned in middle school: I could quickly identify the cool kids and the ones eager for their approval. "One of these things is not like the others," I thought, "and that thing is me."

All the actors wore T-shirts and jeans. Amy Pascal, the head of the studio, dressed casually in a green suede leather jacket, jeans, and fur-lined clogs. The rest of the studio's production executives wore lower-budget versions of Amy's elegant attire. Me? I wore the same thing I did every day: a dark gray suit and a white shirt. Picture a corporate lawyer walking into the offices of Condé Nast.

I spotted Rogen, sharing a joint with Franco in the corner. Rogen had a reputation as a smoker, but this time he may have needed a bit extra to calm his nerves. Everyone seemed jumpy. They all knew the stakes. We'd gathered that day to decide whether to green-light *The*

Interview. In a couple of hours, the team would either begin a rocking new adventure with one of Hollywood's most bankable actors or spend the next few weeks fielding angry calls from agents.

I was the "suit" in a room full of talent and needed to decide that day whether Sony would back Rogen and Franco on their next great adventure.

Normally, the studio never made a decision that way. Contrary to popular belief, studio executives don't read scripts and shout out to their assistants, "I love it. Let's go!" Indeed, Amy and I had pushed Sony in exactly the opposite direction. I believed that in a well-run studio, many factors and many people decide whether to make a movie; you gather the right team—finance, marketing, production, legal, and even public policy—and marry it with the best data.

It is a careful, thoughtful, and sober process that does not involve spur-of-the-moment decisions. People think that it's like one of those frenetic cooking shows where everyone runs around trying to incorporate the secret ingredient. It is actually more like building a large skyscraper, which requires years of financial and construction planning before you even put a shovel in the ground.

Here's the thing about building skyscrapers. Years later, the architects don't remember what the team wore. I remember it all. And, generally speaking, the structural engineer who's in charge of making sure that the whole thing doesn't come crashing down couldn't care less if the rest of the people like him. I cared.

I knew I didn't quite fit in with the actors and moviemakers as they read through *The Interview*, but I didn't consider it a weakness. I viewed it as a strength. They had incredible creative talent. I, on the other hand, had high confidence in the right process to approve movies—even if some frustrated people described the process as "glacial." It can take months, if not years, for a studio to come to a decision, and for the most part, the decision is no.

If you don't use this process, it's easy to lose a lot of money quickly. What appears great in the moment can, on reflection, look like a bad bet. I'd learned this the hard way. The businesses I inherited at Sony were poorly run. When I arrived at the studio, it had weak financial planning, a chaotic green-lighting process, and numerous money-losing businesses it had to jettison. On the creative side, the television production had stalled, the animation slate felt moribund, and many of the movies lost money. I felt good about how the team had turned things around. A better process had helped our bottom line and had led to a couple of hit TV shows such as *The Blacklist* and *Breaking Bad*.

Yet even a good process doesn't guarantee good results. The year prior, the studio had entered the second year of a bad dry spell. We hadn't established another franchise besides *Spider-Man*. The failures had cost us tens of millions. Tired of losing money on tentpole projects, we tried small, edgier productions including *Superbad*—a raunchy, R-rated coming-of-age picture written by Rogen. Bingo! *Superbad* cost about $20 million and took in $120 million at the box office.

Not only had the film made an incredible return, it also opened up a whole new category of movie: the R-rated comedy. Not since the 1980s had anyone thought that this genre had a big enough audience to make it attractive. But demographics had changed, and Rogen had shown the way. He quickly followed with another Rogen adventure, *Pineapple Express*, about a marijuana dealer.

And then we ran into a snag. Rogen had an existing relationship with Universal Studios, which caused a competitive situation when Sony began releasing his films. Both studios vied for his attention, time, and output. Two other factors complicated the situation. First, Amy Pascal and Stacey Snider, the chairwoman at Universal Studios, while friends, had a twenty-year rivalry. Second, Rogen felt that he had to make each movie more and more outrageous to keep his audience engaged. So, when either Stacey or Amy refused to green-light a film because it was too offensive, the other agreed to make it, and guess what? It was inevitably a hit.

Sony found itself in the difficult position of not being able to say no, and Rogen found himself in the enviable position of getting approval of almost anything that he chose to present. An unhealthy dynamic that nevertheless led to a series of financial successes and no material missteps.

Next up on Seth's hit parade: *The Interview*. The table read Sony had requested that day came as no surprise. If Seth wanted a fast decision—to short-circuit the deliberative process through which Sony made most green-light decisions—we wanted to hear the cast read the script. I knew that what reads funny on the page does not always read funny in the room. If it worked, Seth expected a yes on the spot. I was in the room because Amy already wanted to make the movie and we each had to approve all green-light decisions. That left me as the final authority on whether to approve it.

I had been looking forward to this session. While I enjoyed interacting with actors and directors, it happened rarely in comparison to the video calls with the finance team in Tokyo about sexy topics such as amortization policies. It was even rarer that I'd be in the room with the talent when they heard the studio's decision. That job usually fell to Amy.

My attendance raised the expectation of an instantaneous decision, which gave the actors extra energy, and the overall mood a sense of importance. Laughter would determine whether we committed tens of millions of dollars and months of their lives to the project. As soon as the actors started reading, their collective nervousness disappeared. They were hilarious. Rogen and Franco ad-libbed, drew out the best in their fellow actors, and made the rest of the room feel as if they were part of their joyous adventure.

The result was magic. The actors charmed all the executives—myself included. Throughout my tenure as CEO, I had positioned myself as the outsider, the business guy. After just a few minutes, I felt part of the sensuous, vertiginous club of creative talent that pushed boundaries, and I didn't feel beholden to the norms that governed so much of my life.

When the reading was over, Amy jumped up and said, "Let's make this!" And I threw out all of our normal, careful approval processes and found myself agreeing. I joined a fantastic, subversive plot. We rushed into the decision giddy about the project, thrilled to have outflanked our competition at Universal Studios, and, alas, oblivious to the potential ramifications.

There, that was the mistake. I didn't realize it at the moment I made the decision or I would have shouted, "Hold on. Let's think this through!" No, it felt excellent. I felt like one of the gang and, to quote George W. Bush, a "decider."

Twelve months after the table read, the entire company became paralyzed. And then it went straight downhill. A mysterious website invited journalists to type "Die Sony" into any internet browser, where they could find tens of thousands of leaked emails. Emails in which studio executives criticized movie stars. Emails that had sensitive employment contracts.

Then the hackers started releasing employee health records and Social Security numbers. They published pirated versions of upcoming movies such as *The Karate Kid*. They even released the confidential script of the new James Bond movie. That's the ultimate Hollywood sacrilege.

The result was mayhem. Between the constant press coverage of the confidential emails, the destroyed IT system, and the panic over the employee identity theft, the studio became paralyzed.

I had a strong suspicion that the North Koreans had conducted the attack to prevent the release of *The Interview*. For the next five months, the cleanup consumed my life.

If Sony had made a movie about the whole affair and followed Syd Field's framework, the "setup" would feature the decision to green-light the movie, the "confrontation" the hack, and the "resolution" the cleanup. The filmmakers would spend a lot of time on that table read, little on the hack that followed (audiences only want to watch guys at keyboards for so long), and in the "resolution," the audience would witness the pain the hack caused and the team's valiant efforts to set things right.

In reality, the "resolution" mostly involved chaos and lots of law enforcement. That's how Act III of my story began: the arrival of twenty FBI agents. With their brisk efficiency and calm sense of urgency, they gave the appearance of action, but appropriately enough focused on what had happened, not what Sony could do about it. Sony's team, and an army of consultants, worked 24-7 for weeks to get the company back online.

After much forensic investigation, the FBI shared my speculation that the North Koreans had led the attack. Confirmation came later when the North Koreans actually took credit for it.

They didn't exactly love *The Interview*. They didn't love how it satirized their leader, let alone that it ended with his assassination. Their displeasure did not come as a surprise. The harder question is whether I should have predicted how they might express their displeasure.

The summer before the hack, Sony began prerelease publicity for the movie. As we did, the team picked up increasing signs of the North Koreans' discomfort. While no official channel of communication between the United States and the North Koreans existed, we would find vague threats on odd websites. Occasionally, the New York–based North Korean special envoy even gave press interviews to offbeat and obscure news outlets where he voiced his objections to the movie.

Sony didn't ignore what we heard. I checked in with the State Department and experts at the RAND Corporation, a global organization that specializes in research-based analysis. Both told me not to worry. They said North Korea always threatened, but the government was all bark and no bite. That was their experience with Kim Jong Un's father. The son, as it turned out, was another matter. He had only been in power for a couple of years, and no one really understood who he was. It's impossible to overstate the opaque nature of the North Korean regime. The United States has no embassy in Pyongyang; there are no cultural exchanges or business partnerships between the two countries. Even the South Koreans consistently misinterpret their neighbor's statements and actions.

In short, we did have warnings that the North Koreans objected to the movie, but no indication that they would take extreme actions to prevent its release. Should I have handled those warnings differently? Should I have canceled the movie? On balance, I don't think so. There was no precedent of a studio pulling a movie due to the objections of a dictator, and none of the experts warned me of potentially dire consequences such as a hack.

Once the hack occurred, we had to decide whether to release the movie. Many of our employees, who had seen their private lives exposed and, in some cases, their careers destroyed by the hack, vehemently opposed releasing it. They didn't know what more the North Koreans could try, but they had no interest in finding out the answer. Most of them had come to Sony to make light entertainment such as *Jeopardy!* and Will Smith action movies. They didn't care about distributing this movie because "it was the right thing to do."

My bosses in Tokyo had no understanding of why I even wanted to consider releasing it. Unlike me, the Japanese executives didn't feel wedded to principles around free speech that the First Amendment enshrines here. Entertainment companies and newspapers in Japan edit their content because of corporate or government pressure, and no one thinks much of it. Even more important, North Korea represented a real and omnipresent danger to the Japanese. The North Koreans kidnapped children off the streets of Japan in the late 1970s and 1980s and now threatened nuclear war.

I felt terribly conflicted: worried about my employees, respectful of the Japanese perspective, and concerned about my own family. As part of the leaked documents, my daughters' health records had flashed across the internet. I hated that invasion of privacy and the way some journalists had twisted my emails out of context.

Yet, it had also become a matter of principle. The more the North Koreans tried to bully Sony into silencing the movie, the stronger I felt about releasing it.

There is a bit of history here.

When I became CEO at Penguin Group in 1996, the company had not fully recovered from the *Satanic Verses* crisis almost a decade earlier. Iran's Ayatollah Khomeini issued a fatwa ordering Muslims to kill the author Salman Rushdie along with anyone else involved with publishing his novel, including Penguin employees. (Tragically, that fatwa remained in place, and Salman Rushdie was horribly attacked in 2022 in the United States.)

At the time of the initial crisis, my predecessor felt it was important to continue to publish the book and not bow to the Iranian extremists. The publishing industry rallied around Penguin, publishers and booksellers alike. The company spent millions on security, and three people lost their lives (two translators and a bookshop owner). That courageous behavior in support of free speech shaped my belief that releasing the movie was a moral imperative.

It's an example of a schema working well: I had a previous experience that while deeply painful and tragic nevertheless reinforced my belief that open societies rely on the circulation of creative work. *The Interview* was no *Satanic Verses*, but the principle still held.

When Sony wouldn't back down on releasing it, the North Koreans threatened the movie theaters. We were poised to release the movie with millions of dollars spent on marketing when all the major theater companies refused to show it. Conversely, the actors and filmmakers pushed hard for its release. I agreed with the filmmakers' objective but felt that they showed insufficient concern for the threats to their theater partners.

We all felt exhausted and angry. In the midst of these developments, a friend encouraged me to appear on Fareed Zakaria's show to explain the situation. I wanted to present Sony's side of the story—"No, this wasn't just about our IT incompetence; no, we weren't reckless provocateurs." In particular, I wanted to refute an emerging press narrative that we were backing away from releasing the movie. We had to find a distribution partner now that the theaters had refused to show the picture.

I also wanted to divert attention from Amy Pascal, whose emails had led to a world of pain. After hearing encouragement on the idea (the PR team) and objections (my wife), I decided to do it.

A red-eye flight later, I arrived at the New York CNN studio just as the US government confirmed North Korea's culpability for the attack. A few minutes before we were set to record the show, President Obama reacted to the announcement. Standing in the greenroom before our interview, Fareed and I watched as the president boarded Air Force One for his Christmas holiday in Hawaii.

A reporter asked him two questions: What was he going to do about the North Korean attack, and how did he think Sony had behaved until now? Perhaps because he did not have an answer to the first question, Obama answered the second, saying that he was disappointed by Sony's behavior because the company had bowed to the threats by not releasing the movie.

I was stunned. Sony hadn't caved, but the president's comments seemed to confirm a version of events that hadn't happened. I looked down at my phone and saw a text from my wife: "Fuuuuuuuuuuuuuck" (a view consistent with her not having wanted me to sit for the interview). Fareed then offered me a choice: cancel or turn a scheduled ten-minute conversation into an in-depth interview. As I thought about the options, a senior White House official called me to apologize for the president's words. I decided to proceed.

I used the interview to explain, for the first time, what had occurred. I politely differed with Obama; Sony could not release the movie without the theaters' participation, and they definitely weren't participating. Most important, I praised the Sony employees for their extraordinary work throughout the crisis. Then I got back on a plane to LA. The next morning, grateful employees told me that after weeks of being blamed and ridiculed by the media for aiding the cyberattack, they felt heard and appreciated for the first time.

Eventually we released the movie over the internet. Working with Google and Stripe (no other platforms or software companies agreed to help), we did something for the first time: a direct delivery of a movie by a studio to a consumer home.

At the time, the movie's release and the Zakaria interview felt like the end of a monthslong Act III—perhaps the worst few months of my life. While the FBI assured the Sony employees that the North Koreans would not come onto American soil to commit terrorism, they—and also my family—didn't find much comfort in those reassurances. We had heard similar reassurances from people who had said that the North Koreans wouldn't take any action at all.

The threat of terrorism that came after the hack pervaded every aspect of our lives, with health records exposed, compensation plans revealed, critiques of colleagues and stars broadcast over the internet. The employees felt as if their careers could end at any moment due to one leaked email. And, for at least some of them, that was true.

It left everyone—employees, partners, and my family—feeling intensely fragile.

The events we experienced do not fit the definition of trauma—"exposure to actual or threatened death, serious injury, or sexual violence"—but they did leave many of us feeling the same aftereffects since many people understandably took the North Korean threats seriously.[1]

My reactions to that stress followed well-established patterns: I avoided people, places, and things that reminded me of the crisis. I survived by simply turning off my emotions. With the exception of an occasional smile for employees, I found myself staring blankly, reacting mechanically, and just trying to make decision after decision. I experienced numbness punctuated only by feelings of anger and shame.

I felt angry at Julian Assange, who created a wiki of all my emails to make them easily searchable; angry at the press who dumpster-dived into the wiki; and angry at public officials and industry leaders who didn't defend Sony. The mayor of Los Angeles and the attorney general of California never bothered to offer help. The Motion Picture Association of America, to whom Sony paid $20 million in dues every year to "lobby" on the industry's behalf, never jumped into the fight.

Curiously, I never really got angry at the North Koreans, on the assumption that if you kick the hornet's nest and get stung, you can't really blame the hornets.

At first, I focused mostly on disputing the criticism the way I had on Zakaria's show. I couldn't find my way to accept responsibility for green-lighting the movie. Slowly, I came to realize that while I didn't like President Obama's initial criticism about not releasing the movie, he had correctly called the whole idea of the movie a mistake. In fairness, I had realized that the morning of the hack.

For many years I buried it all: the anger, the embarrassment, the shame, the pain my family endured.

Now, as part of writing this book, I have come to believe that the whole affair neither began with that ill-fated table read nor ended with my buried feelings.

The writing made me realize that while I still have anger—toward a few reporters and Rogen, who acted ungratefully to all the Sony employees who had worked so hard to get his movie out—I am even angrier at myself for the suffering my decision caused the Sony employees and my family. Up until that moment, my colleagues had considered me to be cautious and thoughtful; in one reckless moment, I made a decision that harmed them and damaged my reputation.

For years, I had fundamentally believed that the world wished me well, that I had the ability to make good things happen—including keeping my family safe. Then, as a result of the hack, I felt that I had lost those superpowers. I had lost my innocence.

It wasn't a full 180-degree turn, but my family and friends noticed how I had lost some underlying sense of optimism. In psychological terms, I "overaccommodated."[2] That's the term for when some of our fundamental beliefs about the world and ourselves change dramatically in a way that is inaccurate and overgeneralized. My schema had changed. I went from believing one extreme ("the world loves me, and I love it") to another ("the world is scary and wants to hurt me"). Yet again, I responded to the hack in a way that mirrored the responses of trauma survivors. I had used a common, albeit maladaptive, behavior.

Friends say that before the hack I could be quite cynical and biting. I sometimes used to bring to mind a quote from George Carlin: "The reason I talk to myself is because I'm the only one whose answers I accept." An unfortunate combination of arrogance and narcissism given my good fortune and curious state of mind.

Today, having made such a colossal mistake, I feel less judgmental. My schema adapted. Having made such a rash decision, I'm less likely to feel that I have all the answers or to make biting comments about other people's mistakes. I feel more empathetic even when bad decisions hurt me.

The combination of greater empathy and the writing of this book allowed me to reexamine why I green-lit the movie. Sure, I missed the severity of the North Koreans' likely reaction. Yes, I might have allowed commercial imperatives to cloud my judgment. Maybe I felt overconfident based on some recent successes of R-rated comedies.

Looking back on it, I see how the studio made decisions about the Rogen movies more swiftly as the movies succeeded and the studio's confidence grew. The studio believed that the movies couldn't fail—until of course they did.

But there was more. I now remember almost immediately regretting my decision to approve the movie. Within a week I had come to my senses and recognized that this time the writers had gone too far with the subject matter. Each day I thought about asking the filmmakers to modify the ending of the movie by deleting the assassination or rethinking the entire premise, but in the end, we only made a half-hearted proposal to Rogen, which he quickly rejected as too timid. Worse, he accused the studio of cowardice.

I had to choose between going back on my word to make the movie or going along with a movie that already felt like a mistake.

Why didn't I change my mind?

It goes back to that table read. After the read-through, all eyes turned to me for a decision. I was dressed in my dark suit, and part of me resented my parental role. Why did Amy always get to play the role of enthusiast and I had to play the part of the corporate square?

A big part of me enjoyed it. Given that Rogen and Franco clearly did not want my creative input, my authority lay in my ability to say yes or no. There's nothing worse in Hollywood than "broomsticking," which refers to the errands the Wizard assigns Dorothy to put off her realization that he is not a wizard and cannot send her back to Kansas. And there is nothing that expresses power better than a quick decision. I was at once the resentful parent and the "power player." Unsurprisingly, the role of power player felt a whole lot better. I made a decision quickly and recklessly.

Yet even more motivating than the desire to demonstrate power was the desire to be part of the gang.

When I was nine, my parents moved from Scarsdale, New York, to Holland. I did not speak the language and felt desperate to make friends. I fell in with the nerd set—a small group of academically minded boys who came to school with their books in briefcases. We never got invited to parties. To this day, I can remember hearing loud music on a Saturday night from a neighboring house and knowing that many of my classmates were having fun without me.

My parents, who fled Germany at a similar age, had little sympathy for my discomfort. In addition to playing Risk and other board games with my nerdy friends, I found solace at the movies, where the tiny theater's proprietor managed to obtain all the current releases. I fell in love with the glamour and the people that seemed to go with how movies were made. I imagined myself to be part of that community and developed a secret, unexpressed ambition to be a part of that world.

It took me a while to make it, but did I ever. After stops at Penguin, Hollywood Pictures, and AOL, Howard Stringer, the CEO of Sony, called to offer me the job of running Sony Studios. I jumped at the chance.

Once my wife and I settled into Los Angeles, the entire experience started to feel like a cliché. Taking the girls to school, I would bump into Diane Keaton and Cuba Gooding Jr. Celebrities populated the sidelines of the children's soccer games and the aisles of the local supermarket.

As the head of Sony, my opinions mattered to the entertainment community, and as a result my family received treatment that felt unfamiliar: instant access to the hottest restaurants, invitations to the coolest parties and openings, great seats at the Oscars and Golden Globes. It felt as if that kid from Wassenaar had finally arrived. Or had I?

There is always another velvet rope in Hollywood. No matter how exclusive the party, there is always another room that's off-limits. This is true physically and emotionally. And, of course, the coolest people—the actors—hang in the room that's off-limits.

There was a pecking order, and some actors were cooler than others: movie stars trumped successful TV actors, who trumped soap opera stars. Oddly, successful musicians trumped them all. I remember attending the Golden Globes. The room was filled with every TV and movie star you could think of: Julia Roberts, Will Smith, Jerry Seinfeld, they were all there. Then in walks Mick Jagger; the room fell silent in awe.

Despite all their power, studio executives, or "suits," just don't rank. And I was most definitely a suit. The actors treat the suits with deference, but they keep their distance. I once went to the home of Bryan Lourd, a powerful CAA agent, for his annual Oscar party. Daniel Craig, Leonardo DiCaprio, Sandra Bullock, all having a great time with one another—drinking, laughing, singing.

George Clooney, Brad Pitt, and Matt Damon stood talking in a tight circle. I had seen Clooney at the studio that week and went up to join the conversation. While polite, they made clear that I simply did not belong.

I was at the top of the heap in the movie *business* and still felt that I was watching from a folding chair in Wassenaar. I thought that my big studio job would finally change that dynamic. And, to any reasonable outsider, it did. Yet when you really know the landscape, when you can see the patterns within the patterns, you realize that I had broken through on one level and not at all on another.

Perhaps that's what made me so vulnerable during the table read of

The Interview. I had finally broken through to the inner sanctum. For the previous ten years at Sony, I had decided things so carefully and methodically by keeping my ego and emotions out of the equation. Why, then, did I decide something so important so spontaneously? I was trying to belong.

Here's the thing about belonging: the desire to penetrate the inner circle can severely distort your sense of self and the way you make decisions. It's a constant refrain in movies as varied as *Mean Girls* and *The Firm.*

Two schemas conflict in these situations: our experience that conforming to the group increases our acceptance and our experience with the consequences of doing the wrong thing. In extreme versions such as *Brave New World* and *Lord of the Flies*, it can completely uproot the core tenets of a healthy community. Those books reflect a basic human truth that our desire to belong leads us all to weigh heavily the opinions of others.

Lots of studies support what authors have described in novels. In 1951 at Swarthmore College, Solomon Asch conducted what would become one of the most famous studies on conformity.[3] It's 1951, so picture White men, lots of skinny ties, and a deep fear of the "other" due in part to the aura of Senator Joseph McCarthy. (In 1950, he gave his infamous speech in West Virginia claiming that he had a list of known Communists in the State Department.)

Asch recruited a group of volunteers and hired a number of actors. He scripted the actors, and the volunteers thought that the actors were also volunteers. For each experiment, he put several actors and one volunteer in a room. They all looked at the same two cards: One had three lines of varying length marked A, B, and C. The other had only one line, which clearly matched the length of one of the lines on the other card.

He then asked the participants—first four actors, then the volunteer, then two more actors—to state which line on the card with three lines matched the single line on the other card. To the naked eye, the answer was obvious. Then each group of seven repeated the exercise for eighteen trials.

When all the actors answered the question correctly, the volunteers had a 0.7 percent error rate. But in some trials, Asch had the actors give a blatantly wrong answer. Amazingly, 74 percent of the volunteers went along with the wrong answer at least once. When interviewed afterward, some volunteers said that they had initially perceived the lines correctly but came to doubt themselves after listening to the actors. Others said they lied because they didn't want to appear different from the group.

In 2005, Gregory Berns, of Emory University, conducted a version of Asch's experiment in which he scanned subjects with an MRI while they answered the questions. Berns roughly replicated Asch's results.

But wait, there's more: The MRIs for the volunteers who answered inaccurately showed activity in the part of the brain responsible for perceptual processing, suggesting they may actually have seen things differently.[4] Meanwhile, the volunteers who did not go along with the incorrect answers had activation in the amygdala, the emotional center of the brain, which suggests they had an emotional reaction while not conforming.

There are lots of versions of that test that show our desire to go along with the crowd. In 2006, sociologist Matthew J. Salganik and his colleagues created a fake music website where two groups could download previously unknown songs.[5] One group chose songs based on their own opinions. The other group saw how frequently songs got downloaded by others. Unsurprisingly, the group that could see previous downloads chose those songs at a higher rate than the group that chose based only on their own discovery. Yes, recommendations help. We also like going along with the crowd.

From an evolutionary perspective, it's hardly surprising: Would you rather fend for yourself on the plains of Africa or belong to a tribe? How badly do we desire those relationships? UCLA social scientist Naomi Eisenberger has shown that social exclusion can trigger the same neural response as physical pain.[6]

During the table read, I watched as all the other participants saw the script one way—brilliant comedy that built on previously successful implementations of a particular genre. Their insistence, plus my desire to join the cool crowd, made me see it the same way.

Yet, like so many other things that served us well as we evolved, the desire for companionship comes with a heavy price: the inability to know ourselves when buffeted by outside voices. We all accept how peer pressure influences children and adolescents, but, surprisingly, adults make many of the same mistakes.

That's what happened at the table read, and I can still remember the feeling. Everyone in the room reacted in harmony: the movie made them laugh, laughter sells movies, so make the movie. Normally, it was my job to maintain perspective, to see the bigger, more rational picture. When surrounded by others who believed in one answer, I began to believe it too. Just for a moment, I wanted to join the badass gang that made subversive movies. For just a moment, I wanted to hang—as an equal—with the actors. I had grown tired of playing the responsible adult—of watching the party from the outside while I played Risk.

The room of adults acting like teenagers (e.g., lots of weed, juvenile humor, and laughter) activated my schema that gaining acceptance from my peers "required" agreeing with what they wanted. Without realizing it, I felt like that lonely boy in Holland who wanted the affection and respect of his peers. I solved that uncomfortable problem by acting like an adolescent myself; I gave the cool kids what they wanted to gain their acceptance. Unconsciously, I felt that I needed to green-light the movie to achieve that goal. My desire for affirmation overcame all the years of professional training.

The decision to green-light the movie relates to a schema that I'd developed long before the resulting mistake. When I lived in LA, I didn't realize how much I wanted to cross the velvet rope. I didn't grasp how my lifelong desire to belong enticed me to green-light the movie or to concede when Rogen refused my request to remove the assassination. I didn't even realize my long history with FOMO and how that might have affected my behavior.

Now, years later, I find it ironic that while I had requested the table read to understand what emotions the script would elicit in an audience, I had not bothered to examine my own emotional state when walking into that room. My middle school self took over. My adult self lost the courage to disappoint the other kids. The party got out of hand. The company, its employees, my family, and I all paid dearly.

And, yes, all this changed the way I react to certain situations. When confronted by certain kinds of decisions—business or social—I try to understand my true motivation. Especially when I risk feeling motivated to be part of a gang. I used to accept just about every invitation, even if it meant rushing from event to event on the same night. And, yes, as my friends would tell you, I even accepted multiple invitations for the same date *and* time. I optimized for where I would feel least likely to have missed out.

Like many people when they realize something about themselves, I wondered how I had not seen this side of my character years earlier. Especially since so much of what motivated me—the desire to hang with the cool kids—plays a central role in the industry that I helped lead.

As I told my story to Josh, he pointed out that the roots of my FOMO likely developed long before I even went to Hollywood. Shocking: it all comes back to my childhood! My FOMO obviously had deep roots dating back to those lonely days in Holland. Act I clearly influenced both Acts II and III, but the Dutch don't encourage wallowing around in their feelings, and I hadn't ever given myself permission to dig into these emotions.

While it had taken way too long, I felt that I had finally figured out the "why" of my mistake. Yes, I had a strong desire to fit in, but the real problem wasn't FOMO per se. It was that I didn't understand how it affected my decision-making. Joining the gang is okay as long as it doesn't make you approve movies that lead to your company getting hacked. I had never seriously explored my schemas and therefore didn't understand how they affected my decision-making.

While going back and forth on how my schema led to the hack, Josh did the same work to understand how his schemas shaped his decision to keep a diary while serving at the Treasury Department, and how he dealt with the blowback that followed.

4

The Polar Bear

J osh tells his own story:

On July 26, 1994, I woke up early, walked down the six flights of stairs from Antoinette's tiny apartment in Manhattan, caught a cab to LaGuardia, and rushed to make an early flight back to Washington. Starting in late 1992, after I joined the Clinton transition team and then the Treasury Department, I took the shuttle frequently to visit Antoinette in New York. Not as often, as she would rightly point out, as she took the train to see me, but often enough that I knew the protocols and unspoken social cues of that rather run-down yet still-rarefied airport environment.

I felt like *someone* when I took the shuttle. So much so that I used to joke that if I had to die in a plane crash, I hoped it wouldn't be on the shuttle because then I would fall into the category of "others" when the news listed the fatalities. Like all jokes, this one had a ring of truth. At twenty-eight years of age, and after just a year and a half in Washington, my title well outstripped my experience or actual importance.

I pulled out the newspaper as soon as I settled into my seat and, due to the tight quarters, read in small increments on neatly folded pages. Arguably, no institution outside of government mattered more to the people on the shuttle or me than *The New York Times*. The lead headline exhilarated me both as a Jew and as a member of the Clinton administration: "Jordan and Israel Join in Pact Aimed at Broad Mideast Peace." I flipped the paper over to see the articles below the fold. While stories about Whitewater kept coming that year, I had no expectation of finding the next headline. It made me want to vomit: "Treasury Official Is Disavowing Whitewater Details in His Diary." On the front page of *The New York Times*. The story that followed only got worse:

> A senior Treasury official whose diary casts a bad light on the Administration's handling of the Whitewater affair will testify in Congress that his writings do not accurately reflect what occurred. . . . Congressional investigators said today that when Mr. Steiner appeared before Congress next week, he would . . . disavow significant passages in the diary. Mr. Steiner's lawyer, Reid H. Weingarten, said that his client "would not walk away from his diary" but that he would say that the diary did not accurately record what had occurred.

There's a lot to unpack in that paragraph, but to summarize, I had kept a diary that got subpoenaed as part of the Whitewater investigation. The diary included indiscreet summaries about the actions of some of my colleagues. In an effort to exonerate them and extricate myself, I had made a hash of it.

The story was in that sweet spot between deeply embarrassing and utterly humiliating. If you're a staffer, there's nothing worse than becoming the story, especially if it's because you did something incredibly stupid such as write about sensitive subjects in your personal diary. Furthermore, who "disavows" something one wrote oneself?

Michael and I almost didn't know where to begin with my mistake. So many questions popped up after even the most cursory retelling. We decided to start with the most obvious one: Why did I even keep a diary?

In 1988, as my first job out of college, I worked on Governor Dukakis's 1988 presidential campaign. Yes, I was there when he had his picture taken riding a tank only to have that photo used by then Vice President Bush to mock Dukakis's national-security credentials. That ride was a mistake. While the campaign ended poorly, I formed strong friendships with people who ultimately played instrumental roles in my career.

Right after the campaign, I traveled around Asia for four months and kept a journal of my adventures. I kept the diary going through graduate school and a job in New York.

Following Clinton's election as president in 1992, I went to work on his transition team thanks to a friend from the Dukakis campaign. During the transition, I shared an office barely bigger than a Motel 6 bathroom with two much more senior aspiring members of the administration.

At the end of the transition, Roger Altman, who had served in the Carter administration and then had a highly successful banking career, became Clinton's deputy Treasury secretary and offered me a job as his special assistant. My jobs at Treasury, first as executive assistant to the deputy secretary, and then even more so after my promotion to chief of staff to Lloyd Bentsen, the secretary of the Treasury, gave me an intimate view of President Clinton's first two years.

While Whitewater would become the "highlight" of my tenure, it was far from the only interesting thing that occurred during my time at Treasury. In the first eighteen months, I went to Waco, Texas, to visit special agents wounded during the Branch Davidian siege; worked on the appointment of a new Secret Service director; attended a Yomi-uri Giants baseball game in Tokyo with a US trade delegation where the crowd sat in stunned silence as the public announcer pointed out our presence; and flew on Air Force One. Washington life was full of serious projects, vertigo-inducing experiences, and even comic relief through a decent stream of practical jokes.

I wrote about all these events in my diary. There's a long tradition of public officials keeping diaries. While I had no pretension about mine becoming historically important, I had grown up reading histori-cal accounts based on them, everyone from Shackleton's to Churchill's. I had never read about them becoming a source of controversy and embarrassment.

If so many people keep diaries, and so few of them get in trouble, Michael and I decided pretty quickly that keeping the diary did not feel like the key mistake. We had to unpack what happened at least two layers deeper: what I wrote in my diary and how I handled it once it became public.

My diary would never have become public but for the Whitewater investigation, so a little context will help. In our current era, it feels al-most quaint that the Whitewater scandal started with a real estate deal in Arkansas.

In 1978, Bill Clinton was the attorney general of Arkansas and a candidate for governor. His old friends Jim and Susan McDougal in-vited the Clintons to invest in land the McDougals had bought and planned to subdivide in the Ozark Mountains. They called the project the Whitewater Development Corporation.

Like many speculative land deals, it turned out poorly. Interest rates skyrocketed right after the purchase, so their hopes of flipping the land at a quick profit evaporated. So far, so bad, but nothing that, seventeen years later, justified the 1995 congressional hearings that would bear the Whitewater name. Unfortunately for the Clintons, the

McDougals didn't stop at bad investments. They also owned a bank that loaned money to one of their other investments, and when the bank became insolvent, the Resolution Trust Corporation (RTC), a now-defunct governmental agency, became involved. The same RTC that was in charge of cleaning up the savings-and-loan debacle that cost taxpayers tens of billions of dollars.

At its simplest, the Clintons got into business with the McDougals; the McDougals used their bank to lend themselves money; the bank went bust; the agency that cleaned up the mess ultimately reported up to the Treasury Department.

From there the whole saga unraveled in myriad trivial and tragic ways. By the time the Clintons arrived in the White House, various investigations had started and ended and begun again.

Most notably, in his investigation of the Whitewater deal, Ken Starr, the independent counsel, uncovered Clinton's relationship with Monica Lewinsky. And that discovery triggered the president's impeachment.

I had never met Ms. Lewinsky, couldn't have picked Jim McDougal out of a crowd of one, and certainly had no knowledge of what had happened between McDougal and the RTC back in the 1980s, but there I was, or at least there my diary was, on the front page of *The New York Times*, because in 1993, my boss at the time, Roger Altman, had become acting head of the RTC.

Roger, one of the most genuine, thoughtful men you could ever meet, wanted less than nothing to do with the RTC and even less to do with the RTC's investigation of any possible links between Jim McDougal and the Clintons. Roger therefore quickly decided that he wanted to resign as head of the RTC or at a minimum recuse himself on that matter.

Not everyone in the White House liked that idea, and they expressed that view quite vehemently in conversations with Roger. They worried that in his absence an investigation would spiral out of control. And the alternative, an independent counsel, seemed even worse, as that would clearly lead to the excavation of ancient history.

Roger deliberated about the right thing to do and eventually did recuse himself.

Ultimately the whole Whitewater mess bubbled up so badly that the administration decided that they needed an independent counsel after all. And, if you appoint an independent counsel, they investigate. That's what they do—starting by issuing subpoenas to anyone and everyone who might know anything.

I received my subpoena from a Treasury lawyer as I sat in my office overlooking the White House. Today, many great CEOs, especially those who run technology companies, sit in open floor plans surrounded by their teams. Robert Mills, the architect of the Treasury Building, which first opened in 1839, would have laughed at that idea.

Secretary Bentsen's grand corner office faced the White House and the Washington Monument. Next to it, along the side facing the White House, he had a small vestibule with a private elevator so he and his Secret Service detail could go in and out of the building unobserved. Then he had his private dining room. And then there was my office.

In the same way that banks used to build imposing facades and grand halls to assure customers about their stability and solvency, everything about the Treasury architecture gave off a sense of probity and endurance.

I tried to channel that vibe as I read my subpoena. As I realized that it required me to preserve and produce all my papers, letters, calendars, files, and diaries relating to the Whitewater scandal, my mood deteriorated.

When Roger received his subpoena, he immediately called his old friend Dick Beattie, who had served in government and had become chairman at Simpson Thacher, a prominent white-shoe law firm in New York. Dick arrived in Washington the next day to meet with Roger.

After meeting with Roger, Dick generously offered to give me some advice as well. There wasn't much he could tell me beyond what the subpoena stated.

"The Treasury lawyers will take care of any official documents," Dick explained, "but you're responsible for personal ones. You have to look for them and then turn them over. Don't throw anything away. Is that clear?"

"Totally," I answered.

"Do you think that there's anything personal that's relevant for your work?"

I looked Dick calmly in the eye. "Nope. Maybe a reference or two in a letter."

"Great. Then you have nothing to worry about."

Unfortunately, I did. The night before my meeting with Dick, on the day I had received my subpoena, I went home to see whether in fact I had anything relevant.

That night, I frantically turned the diary pages hoping not to find any references to Whitewater. No such luck. There was one action-packed page in tiny, almost illegible handwriting filled with little phrases and descriptions about Whitewater, which ran contrary to parts of how the administration hoped to tell its story.

What I wrote, from a legal perspective, was flawed in any number of ways. Little of it was firsthand knowledge, and much of it was written in a staccato, truncated form. Yet it described various conversations about the investigation, and it clearly cast Roger and the administration in an unflattering light.

So, the night I received the subpoena, I tore that page out of my diary and hid it among other papers. Then I called Antoinette to see if

I had written any letters to her that had mentioned Whitewater. Alas, I'd made that mistake too. Leaving aside the infirmity of love letters that recount Washington controversies, I hadn't even described the situation accurately.

The night after I told Dick that I didn't have anything relevant, I couldn't sleep. In the middle of the night, filled with guilt about the possibility of breaking the law, I imagined the FBI searching my apartment or my having to take a lie detector test about my compliance with the subpoena.

I had all the dark fantasies that crowd your brain at 2:30 a.m. when you've done something you regret. Or, in my case, two things: having written things that could hurt others and then not having confessed to it.

The next day I asked to see Dick again. I explained that I did in fact have something of relevance. When Dick read what I'd written, his facial expression confirmed my fears.

With good reason, Dick seemed shocked that I had written down the White House's opinions on Roger's possible recusal. Alas, I hadn't stopped there. I wrote down other little snippets about the scandal that I'd heard (not witnessed).

I didn't appreciate the extent to which, in the mad cauldron of Washington politics, people say all sorts of dopey things when they're tired, frustrated, or worried. The Clinton White House was no different, especially as it related to the Whitewater investigation, which, with some justification, they considered a politically inspired witch hunt. I should have let their anger wash over me like so many other things that got said in passing. It didn't belong in a diary.

Word to the wise: when you hear the words "independent counsel" or "investigation" or "scandal," don't write about it in your diary.

So, it wasn't really the diary that was the problem, it was clearly what I wrote in it. Keeping a diary can have all sorts of benefits along the lines of other habits such as exercise and good sleep hygiene. I had come to Washington at a young age, but with a bunch of habits already formed. I didn't understand how it made sense to keep some of them (early-morning exercise) and to abandon others. My mistake felt at least partly caused by not understanding something so fundamental as my environment.

Something that works well in one situation may not work in another. The diary I kept in 1989 when surrounded by Bali's swaying palm trees, a diary that combined scattered impressions and even a little terrible poetry, helped me process judgments and observations.

Now fast-forward to 1993 and the Treasury Department. At the age of twenty-seven, I had a job that usually goes to someone far more experienced. How did I process that experience? Alas, with the same technique that had helped me in the highlands of Papua, Indonesia.

Michael and I felt that we had figured it out: I made a mistake during Act II by not understanding my environment. Not quite.

Shortly after I received my subpoena, I realized that I needed my own lawyer. There's a cottage industry of Washington lawyers who help government officials and corporate executives navigate through federal investigations and congressional hearings. I needed someone who could anticipate the likely questions, handle press inquiries, and provide some psychological support.

I ended up hiring Reid Weingarten, an up-and-coming litigator, who eventually went on to become, according to *The National Law Journal*, International Business Crime Defense Lawyer of the Year for six consecutive years. Years later, he represented everyone from Bernie Ebbers to Roman Polanski. Great company.

Early on, Reid explained that for people such as me, people who acted stupidly (e.g., keep written records that get disclosed) and hadn't witnessed anything illegal, big investigations can become perjury traps. From the moment the process began to the time it petered out, I testified under oath about ten times. Each time I had to swear to tell the truth; each time I tried to answer nearly identical questions using nearly identical language.

For the first few interviews, which took place in dreary, battered conference rooms, I felt intense anxiety as I tried to reconcile what I had written and what I remembered. The diary had none of the nuance that would have made the passing comments in it seem far less consequential.

My efforts to describe that complexity appeared tortured. The investigators—some congressional staffers, others FBI agents, a few federal prosecutors—would ask a question; I'd answer it; then they would quote a diary entry or a letter I had sent to Antoinette. They used the quotes to suggest that I hadn't answered their question truthfully; I'd explain that my diary or letters weren't meant to be precise accounts of what had occurred; they'd ask if I was lying to my diary or lying to them; I would say neither; they would make a sarcastic comment; my lawyer would intervene. Rinse and repeat.

All the interviews came in preparation for three "big" events: testimony before Senate and House committees, and before the grand jury impaneled by the special prosecutor. By the time I got called before the grand jury, I was fairly inured to the process and no longer worried about the questions or my answers. The interviews had taken on the semblance of theater: everyone knew their lines.

The grand jury testimony came first. The independent counsel had let reporters know the appearance dates of key witnesses, so a couple of TV reporters lined the sidewalks shouting questions at me as I walked into the courthouse.

My testimony took place in private before fifteen or so bored-looking Washingtonians. I was no Hillary Clinton, and their attention level showed it. I walked out relieved that it was over and dreading what would come next: testifying in front of the Senate.

A year after I became chief of staff—a year spent trying to prove that Secretary Bentsen had made a wise choice appointing someone so young—I appeared before the Senate Banking Committee. The mere fact that I had to appear could not have run more directly against the dignified, ethical, understated approach to governing that Secretary Bentsen espoused.

No one was happy with me as I arrived before the committee. Members of the Clinton administration, including some of my closest friends, felt angry that I had kept a diary filled with easily misinterpreted comments. Members of Congress, most notably several Republican senators, felt convinced that I was lying about my diary to cover up a cover-up.

I raised my right hand to take my oath before a phalanx of photographers and a scowling row of senators. C-SPAN carried it live; the networks played it heavily on the evening news. The Republicans had blown up excerpts from my diary that they made me read aloud. The Democrats tried to get me to disavow what I had written.

The senators asked detailed questions about events I could barely remember. I often reverted to a stock response: "Senator, I do not recall."

I didn't break down in tears or, like Albert Brooks in *Broadcast News*, start to sweat uncontrollably. I also didn't convince anyone that I could truly reconcile what I thought had happened and what I had written.

When the hearing ended, Senator Ben Nighthorse Campbell came up to me and said, "That which doesn't kill you makes you stronger." I felt pretty dead but definitely didn't feel any stronger.

Sure, I hadn't caused any of the underlying issues that provoked the Whitewater investigation, but I sure as hell hadn't made the situation any better. I had caused myself and people I cared about a world of pain.

I felt terrible about hurting the administration and particularly so about the damage I had done to Roger. Because we wanted to avoid even the appearance of collusion, Roger and I didn't discuss the investigation or its impact. We interacted several times a day on other Treasury business yet couldn't discuss the one thing that weighed on us most heavily.

Beyond apologizing to Roger, I couldn't explain how I had attempted to mitigate the damage by explaining to the investigators that my diary didn't capture the essence of what had transpired. I hoped that the testimony would allow the public and, even more important, my colleagues to understand what had happened. I had definitely not succeeded. At best, I had helped coin a new word: "liary"—a diary where you lie to yourself.

In the aftermath of my testimony, many observers mocked me for keeping a diary, while others—some publicly and many others privately—questioned my decision to turn it over to the investigators. Savvier players doubted that the investigators would ever have known about it or the letters to Antoinette if I hadn't produced them. The FBI obviously had better things to do than search my apartment.

I don't regret turning it over. I realized early on that there's a big difference between acting stupidly and acting illegally.

I do, however, regret having tried too hard to mitigate the diary's damage by hedging and modifying, explaining and interpolating what I had written. While I never lied to the investigators, I also didn't just own it. I should have followed that old adage: "Never complain, never explain."

Instead, in an effort to protect my colleagues, and to ameliorate their unhappiness with me, I drew additional attention to what I had written. I tried to recharacterize what I had written or add additional context around it. I said that what I wrote wasn't meant as a verbatim account, that I had jotted down my impressions. All those explanations understandably sounded as if I were disowning what I myself had written. Something about my personality made me too eager to please my colleagues, too concerned about their reactions. I acted out of loyalty and embarrassment and just made it worse. One news story quoted an anonymous White House source asking how I "could have done something so f—ing stupid."

My notoriety declined quickly. While the testimony did little to assuage my colleagues' anger or convince the Republicans that I had acted truthfully, I survived. Secretary Bentsen graciously declined my resignation offer, so I kept working away on issues that mattered more and generated far less attention.

Washington has a short memory for scandals that don't topple presidents or involve sex. But the world's losing interest didn't mean that I could move on emotionally.

When you're in the midst of a crisis or scandal, it feels as if the whole world is obsessed with it. Almost always, the person in the middle of the storm overestimates how much people pay attention to it. That's called the spotlight effect, reflecting that sometimes we disproportionately feel that everyone is watching us. As Seneca put it, "There are more things . . . likely to frighten us than there are to crush us; we suffer more often in imagination than in reality."[1]

Unfortunately, in the Washington fishbowl, sometimes that sense of vulnerability isn't all wrong. At restaurants, I felt that people stared at me, and some people did—although with far less frequency than my imagination suggested. At times it took on a comic aspect. I once overheard a man drop my name as a way of trying to impress his date. I began to think that because one guy talked about my diary in a restaurant, others must be doing so as well. So I retreated and reduced my already-modest social engagement.

My inner dialogue was exhausting. "Are people making fun of me? If so, why do I care? Of course, I care!" And on and on. In psychological terms, I was overgeneralizing. People who overgeneralize can think that ambiguous stimuli—such as someone glancing in your direction—are evidence of a broader phenomenon. In my case, I thought everyone knew who I was and thought negatively of me.

Even my apartment didn't completely protect me from that tendency. One night, blaring music from the apartment below woke me at 1:00 a.m. Roused from badly needed rest, I tried a pillow over my head, then earplugs, then reading. All to no avail. The time had come to confront my neighbors. Yet I hesitated. I had no doubts about the righteousness of my complaint. Still, I had trouble acting.

I felt, in those moments, that the crisis had overwhelmed all other aspects of my life, so I lay in bed getting angrier at myself, angrier at the reporters who had written about me, and angrier at my neighbors. As William Godwin wrote, "The invisible things are the only realities."[2]

I couldn't take it any longer.

In bare feet, sweatpants, and a T-shirt, I barreled down the stairs ready to demand that the person turn down the fucking music. I knocked. No one answered. I knocked again.

Finally, a happy-looking teenager opened the door. "Hey. What's up?"

"Would you mind turning down the music a little, please?" I asked politely.

"No problem, dude," the boy replied—without a glimmer of recognition of me or my diary.

I went to sleep relieved to be just another ancient adult. When you feel ashamed, anonymity washes over you like a warm, comforting shower.

At times, my shame migrated to anger, which extended well beyond unruly neighbors. I dwelt too much on reporters who had, I felt, mistreated me, colleagues who had not expressed sufficient support, and politicians who had used my situation to score partisan points.

I had revenge fantasies that far exceeded in scale any possible damage that others had caused me. I used their actions—most of which were well within the norms of their respective professions—as an excuse not to examine my own. I assigned motives to people who had barely given me a thought instead of trying to figure out why I had done what I did.

During a particularly tough grilling about whether she should have known more about her Whitewater real estate investment, First Lady Hillary Clinton answered, "Shoulda, coulda, woulda." Who hasn't felt that way after making a bad mistake?

"Shoulda" done something differently: in retrospect, we know what we should have done.

"Coulda" done the right thing: no one stopped us from acting in a way that would have prevented so much discomfort.

"Woulda" chosen a different path: if we had known the pain the decision would cause, we might have acted differently.

When we make mistakes, we immediately wish we had made better choices; we want to wind back the clock. The regret we feel about our decision, especially when it's amplified by a chorus of criticism, quickly leads to embarrassment, guilt, and shame.

I felt all three during the months of testimony and press coverage. When my diary got exposed, I immediately got chastised for breaking the norms that govern behavior in Washington (e.g., watch what you write in your diary or don't be so naive as to turn it over).

That criticism had a deep impact because it related closely to what gets imprinted on children as young as two years of age. Even very little children can distinguish between themselves and others, which allows them to feel positively (e.g., pride and gratitude) or negatively (e.g., embarrassment and guilt). Those reactions are partly what drive healthy social behaviors and interactions.[3]

When my mistake damaged my reputation, embarrassment followed. It hurts, sometimes badly, to face criticism, especially when that pain relates to how we're perceived. It changes our relationships with the people who witness our mistakes. As Jessamyn West wrote in *To*

See the Dream, "It is very easy to forgive others their mistakes; it takes more grit and gumption to forgive them for having witnessed our own."[4]

At the same time that I felt embarrassed, I also felt deeply guilty. The criticism amplified my self-judgment. I knew I had hurt my colleagues and more generally added to the Whitewater distraction. My apologies helped—especially to the people with whom I worked most closely. Even without having read the relevant literature I knew how apologies can lead to forgiveness and reconciliation.

In the end, however, while the fading attention led to less embarrassment and the apologies helped me feel less guilty, my shame lingered. Unlike guilt, which reflects the belief that we did something wrong, shame comes from believing that something is wrong with us.[5] Importantly, unlike embarrassment, shame can come from private acts where we assume how others would react if they knew about what we did.

At its most severe, "feeling ashamed induces the sentiment of worthlessness, inferiority and incompetence, and often leads to a want to escape and withdraw socially."[6] Rather than feeling empathy for others, it can drive us to look increasingly inward and feel badly about ourselves.

When we feel ashamed, we tend to think that everyone disapproves of us. We overgeneralize, which makes us feel as if a few snide comments or unappealing posts on social media reflect a broader truth about how we're perceived. We assume that the whole world has witnessed our mistake and cast its judgment. That form of overgeneralizing, which can get compounded by the spotlighting effect that I experienced, can lead to isolation, and opting out of the activities about which we're ashamed. The more we opt out the more likely it becomes that we obsess about them.

Just because we avoid those situations doesn't mean we stop thinking about the problem. In his journal, Henry David Thoreau wrote, "To regret deeply is to live afresh."[7] For most of us it feels more like "dying again."

It's so hard not to think again and again about a really bad mistake. It's a little like food poisoning: well after the bad oyster has left your system, the thought of oysters can still cause discomfort.

That's called ruminating, and among other problems it makes us preoccupied with the gap between our ideal selves and the way we actually act.[8] We beat ourselves up over our imperfections; we take an isolated event in which we exhibited one particular trait and blow that trait out of proportion. We not only generalize about what others think, we also overgeneralize about ourselves: I lied in this context, therefore, I'm untrustworthy.

"Chatter" is a popularized way of describing rumination, which takes the form of an unhelpful voice in our head. Studies have shown how it hurts student performance on tests, causes stage fright, and even undermines business negotiations.[9]

All of that chatter and rumination drives anxiety: the feeling in the pit of your stomach where shame and guilt get egged on by a mean-spirited inner voice. At its worst, it consumes a vicious amount of emotional energy, interrupts sleep, and drives away the emotions that might actually help.

My unwillingness to confront my neighbor captures so many elements of this spiral. I had moved beyond the guilt about how my diary had hurt others to feeling ashamed about myself. Guilt felt specific: I felt badly about the problems my diary had caused for others. Shame felt general: Did my keeping a diary mean that I had generally poor judgment? Had I forfeited my ethical standing by trying too hard to protect my colleagues?

In the fog of the early-morning hours, I felt that I had developed a terrible new schema where I had no moral authority. How did I have the right to criticize others given my own predicament?

My shame made me anxious about taking actions that risked reminding me of the source of my discomfort. I therefore lay in bed ruminating about how the diary had deprived me of the moral authority to enforce basic neighborly norms. The more I ruminated, the more anxious I became. My anxiety magnified the "risk" of the confrontation. Then I felt ashamed for feeling anxious. Only someone in that kind of spiral would think that teenagers playing music too loudly in the middle of the night would care about my diary.

By avoiding situations where I might feel judged, I didn't find out that others had no intention of judging me and most likely didn't even know anything about the diary. By avoiding, we allow the anxiety to fester, which only increases its toxicity.

When rumination increases anxiety, it's no surprise that we often resort to suppression: we try not to think about the subject at all. That's hard because "suppression is a street battle raging in the forefront of the mind, not a few random muggings hidden deep in its alleyways."[10]

Initially, it can feel like a constant effort to block the memories of the shame. We do it internally by suppressing them and externally by avoiding people and activities that might trigger the memories. Opting out feels like self-care. While intuitively suppressing the events and pain feels like a good coping strategy, everyone from novelists to scientists has recognized that it just doesn't work.

As soon as I left Washington, I tried to cram Whitewater into the darkest corner of my mind. I skipped articles about it, failed to see the humor in jokes about it, and avoided anything close to a serious examination of what had happened or how I felt about it. As a result, it didn't disappear; it just popped up at inopportune moments. I couldn't read an article that referenced diaries without fear that mine would get mentioned. By avoiding these articles, my fear of them only increased. While others had clearly moved on from my saga, it remained huge in my imagination.

For years, when I thought about my diary, it felt as if all the action happened during Act II: I just shouldn't have written down what I did. I simply didn't appreciate the context in which I was operating. That's certainly true. Then, after Michael and I discussed it, we felt as if it all would have been better if I had understood that my schema, which developed before I wrote in my diary, made me too eager to stay in the good graces of my colleagues. I should just have owned what I wrote and not allowed myself to worry so much about how people would react to it.

I've finally come to realize that it's actually an Act III story: what happened after I left Washington. I had tried way too hard for too many years not to think about my polar bear. The word "diary" led me to change the subject; I associated publicity with appearing before Congress. Writing this book served as an intense form of exposure therapy: I had to talk repeatedly about what had happened and why.

The process made the whole experience feel much less weighty and made me appreciate that I had carried the story long after others had forgotten it. Like confronting a bully, the story lost some of its power when I addressed it directly.

It also allowed me to forgive myself. The people I had hurt had accepted my apologies at the time. The damage I had caused the Clinton administration felt relatively inconsequential in hindsight. That doesn't minimize the mistake or suggest that I hadn't caused unnecessary pain. It simply highlights that forgiveness and self-forgiveness help shorten the half-life of shame. They help us realize the universality of our imperfections.

I wish I had had more empathy for myself and felt less shame. Suppression clearly didn't work. Like a hand pushing through the dirt of a shallow grave in a bad horror movie, my diary kept inserting itself into my life.

I should have realized that an alternative approach stared at me day after day. In the bookcase of my study, I have only one souvenir from Washington. It's not a photo with President Clinton or one with Secretary Bentsen on a foreign trip. It's a small, framed clipping of a newspaper photo with a Post-it attached to the corner. The clipping shows a stuntman engulfed in flames as he runs down the street. The Post-it has only three lines:

To: Josh
From: Roger C. Altman

I wondered if you'd seen this photo of me?

Roger, who acted with such grace and generosity through the whole unhappy investigation, gave me the clipping during the worst of the Whitewater drama. The man I hurt the most with my diary had the perspective to find humor in the controversy, the generosity to maintain our friendship, and the wisdom to confront the situation head-on.

PART 2

You're
Not
Alone

5

The Life Cycle of Mistakes

By telling and retelling our stories—in addition to driving each other a little crazy—we had gained a much clearer sense of what had happened and why. Through iteration and research, we began to believe that our mistakes—while unique—fit a broader pattern.

We wanted to test our hypotheses with a larger group of people who had made their own mistakes. In addition to learning about their mistakes, we also had to learn how to talk about mistakes.

When listening to someone describe a triumph, enthusiasm and curiosity work well. If the story relates to failure, admiration and sympathy play important roles. We found that eliciting stories about mistakes required us to develop different skills.

Since it annoyed us when we got asked about our mistakes, we initially didn't feel comfortable asking other people about theirs. Sure, when it came up organically, we didn't mind listening to people spill the tea. Who doesn't like a little gossip? But it felt unseemly to press ahead with questions about what had caused someone else to feel horrible.

So, we had to find a way to talk about mistakes that didn't suggest that we wanted gossip and did respect the pain people had experienced. That required trust: first of ourselves, then each other, and then from the people we interviewed. We needed them to talk about how they felt, not just what had happened. The stories you'll read therefore aren't investigations. No one wants to open up to an inquisitor. We didn't seek third-party perspectives on what happened. We know that memories can play terrible tricks on the mind, but we weren't trying to find out the "true" facts. When you see quotes without other attributions, they all come from the subject of the chapter. Each person reviewed what we wrote about her or him. That doesn't mean that people always agreed with it, but they had a chance to correct what we wrote and suggest edits.

Building trust required us to avoid rushing to judgment or a conclusion. When we first heard stories, we often thought we understood within the first few minutes of a conversation what had happened. We had to control the urge to present our "answer" too quickly. Just as we had difficulty going from never speaking about our mistakes to writing about them openly, we also edged our way into writing about others. Indeed, we needed to postulate less and question more. As you'll read in Rosana's chapter, we began to ask "Why?" more frequently.

There's a temptation when listening to someone else's story to interject with self-referential anecdotes. While they help demonstrate empathy, rarely do they have sufficient commonality to help illuminate the underlying puzzle. It took us a while to overcome that inclination.

A brief note on whom we interviewed. We began having informal conversations with close friends. Then we asked people to examine their mistakes in a series of long, in-depth interviews. Some of the stories we heard ended up in headlines, and others felt both private and deeply universal. Each person with whom we spoke owned her or his mistake, which required bravery and a genuine desire to understand *why* it happened.

Everyone makes mistakes. And everyone makes mistakes that impact their lives and from which we can learn. For many people, those consequences are profound and sometimes deeply unfair. This is not a book, however, about how inequitably society treats mistakes.

We also didn't pursue stories about mistakes that led to deep emotional or physical trauma, although some came close. Mistakes that result in horrific car crashes are a kind of tragedy that merit separate investigation.

Conversely, some mistakes can have happy and serendipitous outcomes. We avoided those. As the legendary restaurateur Danny Meyer said, "The road to success is paved with mistakes well handled."[1] That's true, and there are many great examples in his and other books.

If you're curious about those kinds of stories, start with the invention of Post-it Notes—how an accidental discovery led to a ubiquitous product. Instead, we focused on people who considered themselves to be fortunate, but rather than writing about what made them happy or successful, we focused on a moment when they wished they had acted differently.

That's where almost all these stories started when we first heard them: the moment when they made the mistake. As you'll read in the stories that follow, however, these mistakes constitute a tiny moment in longer, richer lives. Yes, moments of intense consequence, but basically incomprehensible without the broader context. We came to realize that the story of the mistake almost always ran much deeper than the moment it happened.

In some cases, the mistakes reflected the schemas people brought to that moment. You'll read about how those schemas—and ignorance of them—led to crises. Something that happened in the past leads to a bad decision. What happens before the mistake makes all the difference. That was true for Michael.

In other cases, we heard how what happened during the mistake led to a bad decision. Josh's decision to keep the same kind of diary in Washington that he had kept while backpacking around Asia demonstrated that he hadn't adjusted to his surroundings. Some of the stories relate exactly to the problem of not knowing, or adjusting insufficiently to, the context. It's one that we all experience in day-to-day life. Just think about the stress of trying to figure out the right clothes to wear to a party: casual, semiformal, or formal. Not knowing the context can lead to embarrassment.

Finally, what happens after the mistake can make it far more consequential than the actual decision would merit. Josh's suppression of the diary drama prevented him from experiencing his emotions. Without that process, he couldn't get to the next stage: self-forgiveness. Surfacing the painful emotions would have motivated him to figure out what had really happened and allowed him to let it go. If only he had talked about it more, the diary would have come to bore him as much as it certainly did his friends.

None of this should suggest that we no longer have regrets. We deeply wish we had not green-lit the movie or kept a diary. Talking about our mistakes did mean that we could place these decisions in their broader contexts. This helped us think more expansively about how to unpack what had really happened to us and the people with whom we spoke. Their stories both affirmed part of what we discovered and highlighted what we had missed as we tried to understand the role mistakes play in all our lives.

The following stories demonstrate that while mistakes do follow patterns, each of us experiences those patterns differently. We hope that the stories will help you identify the patterns that lead to your mistakes and encourage you to talk about them with the same openness as the people we interviewed.

Their generosity encouraged us to reexamine what we had understood about our mistakes. Their honesty helped us destigmatize what had previously caused shame and gave us permission to disclose what we thought we had to hide. These stories reinforced our belief that mistakes provide a through line across every stage of life.

6

The Front Row

Tony Schwartz works with leaders around the world to help them manage their energy by better understanding what's in their way physically, emotionally, and mentally. Through books, speeches, leadership programs, and consultations, he provides insights into what internally blocks us and the stories we tell ourselves when challenged. For all the passion he brings to his subject, Tony's demeanor and success make him exactly the kind of person you would *not* expect to lose his cool in front of an audience.

Many years ago, a company asked Tony to speak to a group of high-potential young leaders about the power of absorbed attention, and the myth that multitasking increases efficiency. As Tony paced the front of the room and scanned the audience, he saw heads nodding and basked in the mix of appreciation and laughter. Everyone seemed engaged.

Everyone except one young man in the front row who avidly scribbled on his phone. Worse still, Tony noticed that the man wore earphones and occasionally seemed to be mouthing words. Tony assumed that the man was catching up on emails or texts. Perhaps he was even listening to music—and singing along silently as he did. As much as Tony tried to focus on his talk, he felt himself getting more and more upset.

Finally, and impulsively, he walked over to the man and grabbed the phone out of his hand. As Tony held it up to the audience, he said, "This is exactly the problem I'm talking about. It's not possible to do two things at the same time."

Tony and the man locked eyes. To Tony's surprise, he noticed that the man seemed remarkably unembarrassed.

"Why don't you take a look at what's on the screen?" he said calmly. Tony looked down at the phone, only to find nearly verbatim notes of his speech.

"So, what about the earphones?" Tony asked.

The man hesitated. "Are you sure you want to know?"

"Yes," Tony heard himself reply sheepishly, instantly realizing that he should just have cut his losses.

"Well, I served in the military. On my last tour in Afghanistan, I led a scouting mission with my troops along a road. While we rested, I bent down behind a tank to tie my boots. Just as I did, one of my soldiers stepped on an IED. It exploded, killing him instantly, and injuring several other soldiers. I didn't get injured because I was behind the tank, but the explosion pierced my eardrums and left me hard of hearing. I'm wearing hearing aids, and I also read lips."

Tony felt a sickening wave of embarrassment wash away the positive energy that had animated the first part of his talk. He apologized.

So, what exactly went wrong?

For starters, it's not great to grab anyone's phone, and particularly not for an experienced speaker to do it in front of a large audience.

The deeper mistake related to Tony's conviction about what he'd observed. He got the facts right: the young man clearly looked engrossed in his phone, had some sort of device in his ears, and was silently mouthing words. Just not for the reasons Tony assumed.

In fairness, with those facts most of us would make assumptions similar to Tony's. That's a simplistic schema: "person on a phone during a speech probably equals someone who's multitasking." Because of Tony's longtime interest in what motivates people, however, he recognized that he had reacted so strongly for another reason. Tony believes that humans aren't satisfied with facts by themselves and feel compelled to make meaning from them, which is another way of describing how our early experiences shape our schema.

By his own telling, Tony grew up feeling neglected by his parents and left to fend for himself. As he grew older, he sought affirmation and reassurance from others—especially through his achievements. His early experiences fueled his ambition but also left him feeling vulnerable to slights—to any sense of feeling unseen.

"After food and water," Tony told us, "the most important survival need for any child is to feel worthy and valuable. When that's not met—as it wasn't for me—you carry the feeling into adulthood. My career has focused on helping leaders spend less time trying to defend and assert their value so they can invest more time creating value."

Part of what makes Tony compelling as a writer and a speaker is the intensity of his convictions. But his childhood experiences also make him vulnerable to interpreting difficult encounters through the narrow lens of his lifelong fear of not being good enough. "In a way, I've taught what I needed to learn. For all the work I've done on this issue, I'm not immune to these feelings."

Tony's ongoing self-inquiry—and his growing capacity to acknowledge difficult feelings—has changed the way he reacts to situations when he doesn't get the external acknowledgment he long believed necessary.

Tony's ability to identify the schema that drove his mistake is a measure of the work he's done to understand what drives him. Both of us, and most of the people with whom we spoke, did not make that identification until after having gone over their mistakes again and again.

Many of us experience so much pain from the consequences of our mistakes that we rationalize them away or find others to blame for them. In other cases, we write off our mistakes as onetime lapses and assume that there isn't anything much to learn from them. When our embarrassment, shame, and regret are too big, we may even completely suppress the memory of a mistake altogether.

Each story that follows is different, but all of them had the same genesis: a mistake that caused shame and regret. While the cadence differs, they all share the same pattern: the revelation of an embarrassing mistake followed by a realization that the real story often differed from what people had told themselves for many years.

"Feelings of inadequacy still arise for me," Tony told us, "but less often, less intensely, and for shorter periods of time. The more I've been able to accept all of who I am—for better and for worse—the less I've had to defend myself. And no, I've never again grabbed anyone's phone."

7

The Lunch Box

Rosana Kapeller is a renowned biologist and the first-ever life sciences entrepreneur-in-residence at Google Ventures. She radiates warmth, optimism, and curiosity, laughs easily, and speaks fluent English tinged with a Brazilian Portuguese accent.

Just below that approachable exterior lies a mind that developed theories on how dark genomes could hold valuable clues for drug discovery. Her biography includes words that only scientists understand. She is, in short, very smart, and she's had serious financial success. Yet, aside from the elegant Cartier watch on her wrist, you would never guess just how much money she has made.

There's no pretense, no artifice, just the unbridled enthusiasm of a woman who can't quite believe that the world has rewarded her so generously for work that she loves and given her the blessing of a thirty-year marriage and lovely children.

It's therefore hard to imagine that she's haunted by a terrible mistake, but she is. Something that took years to get over. Here are two events from her life. Which one do you think is the mistake that caused so much regret?

Rio, Brazil, 1967. Four-year-old Rosana walks into her family's apartment proudly swinging her new lunch box. It swishes past her school uniform. In the living room, she sees her father—evidently exhausted from the stress of running the family's media empire—lying on a couch. A thought crosses her mind: "What would happen if I smashed my lunch box onto my father's head?" Moments later, blood gushes from her father as he stares at Rosana in disbelief.

Cambridge, Massachusetts, 2001. Rosana quits her job at Millennium Pharmaceuticals to cofound Aileron Therapeutics, a company that ultimately goes public.

Hint: Her father recovered quickly from the blow to the head. She was only four years old, after all. The Aileron story didn't end nearly as well.

To understand Rosana's path from Rio to chief scientist at a fast-growing biotech company, you have to go back in time. All the way back to 1923 and Rosana's great-aunt in Vienna.

Regina Kapeller-Adler, age twenty-three, received her doctorate in chemistry from the University of Vienna. For the next ten years, because of her gender and religion (Judaism), she could work only as an unpaid researcher. Then, in 1934, she discovered an innovative pregnancy test that led to international recognition. Her career took off.

Just when she hit her stride, the Anschluss rolled into Austria, which forced Kapeller-Adler and her husband to flee the Nazis. They settled in Edinburgh, where she got her Doctor of Science, worked in the Royal Infirmary during World War II, and ultimately had a long, distinguished career teaching and seeing patients.

Rosana heard this story in her childhood. The story of a fierce female scientist who made remarkable discoveries; a woman who did not allow language barriers, immigrant status, and prejudice to stop her from building a hugely successful career.

It wasn't the only successful-immigrant story Rosana heard growing up. Her immediate family had fled Ukraine before settling in Brazil in the 1920s. There they started Grupo Bloch, a media conglomerate, which ultimately owned radio and television stations across the country.

At an early age, Rosana decided that she would follow the lead of her great-aunt. "I knew since I was twelve that I wanted to be a scientist." Commerce and science and fearlessness swirled around in the young woman's head.

When she imagined her future, she slowly came to realize that it required a more technical education than she could find in Brazil. She moved to Boston, partly for love—a man who eventually became her husband—and mostly to pursue her PhD. Boston was home to the first industrial revolution in the United States (textiles), and to the second (technology), and Rosana arrived at the launch of a movement that would match the first two in importance: biotechnology.

By the time she graduated from Tufts, the movement had begun. The first few companies—Genentech, Biogen, Cetus—grew out of the major research universities on the East and West Coasts. Rosana chose to join Millennium Pharmaceuticals, where she ultimately became the director of the molecular and cellular biology department. Under her leadership, the team worked to validate the function of genes.

It was an exciting moment in genetics. "This was the period of sequencing the genome. We identified them but had no idea what they really did. What was their function? How can we assay them? How are any of these genes going to be drug targets?"

She excelled at the science and grew into a serious manager—if not an adept bureaucrat. A sad fact that she learned when her boss left. "I thought that I should be her replacement. Other people in the team thought I should be her replacement. I was very arrogant. She selected somebody else, someone who was older, who had more experience, who knew how to operate, and knew how to manage up.

"I was not very good at managing up. I didn't know how to play politics or be nice. I would just say to people, 'Here, this is yellow, and it's yellow. You think it's green? It's not green. It's yellow. Take it or leave it.' I wasn't very good. It wasn't very subtle."

In science, leadership experience often starts "late," after years of training. In Rosana's case, she attended medical school, then got her doctorate, then did bench science at Millennium; so she was forty-two when she got passed over. She didn't take the decision well after ten years of service.

"I was pissed. I wasn't that young. So that was my mindset: I'm tired of being a cog. I'm tired of if they say, 'Jump,' I ask, 'How high?' I didn't see an opportunity for progress, so therefore, why am I staying here? I'm a scientist. So my goal was to be VP of research." She wanted to be the chief scientist—the ultimate decider on the research and its applications.

There was just one problem: she had never served in that position, and her previous experience hardly made her an obvious hire for it given her lack of leadership credentials.

The résumé version of her life before her mistake comes into clarity: incredibly smart woman leaves Brazil, gets her PhD, achieves professional success, but longs for a greater challenge. What we've learned about schemas, however, suggests that our approach to life runs far deeper than what appears on LinkedIn.

She needed a company that would take a risk on her. "Looking back, there was no way in the world that particular start-up could hire someone experienced because nobody would work with them! They had to get someone who was inexperienced."

By definition, however, that meant her taking a risk as well. When "underqualified" people get jobs that seem beyond their reach, it should probably make them anxious about their employer. Groucho Marx expressed a version of that concern when he resigned from the Friars Club, stating, "I don't want to belong to any club that would accept me as one of its members."

Rosana's eagerness for the right position overcame any natural reservations partly because despite knowing so much about so many things, Rosana didn't know much about how to perform due diligence on a biotechnology start-up.

She couldn't fully see herself or her environment. To make good decisions, we need to know both the situation and our frame of mind. Her anger from getting passed over at Millennium clouded her judgment, drove her desire to move quickly, and led her to focus excessively on getting a title that included the word "chief."

"I cared about the science. That science was good. Everything else was not." She did not understand the situation she joined: the poor financial position and the risk of getting layered by a new boss. Why, beyond inexperience, had she not investigated the opportunity more carefully? Partly because she had a schema about risk-taking that made her believe she could drive a successful outcome. This wasn't the first time in her life that she'd acted out of conviction rather than evidence—unusual behavior for a scientist. When she'd moved to Boston, it was to be with a man with whom she'd only had a brief relationship while they both visited Israel. Importantly, however, that man became her husband, so she had experience with impulsive decisions working out well.

"I was the kind of person who left my family at twenty-three and moved in with a guy who I had seen a total of four and a half months in my life. I abandoned a family that was a cocoon with a lot of support and said, 'See you later!' I came to this country with nothing in terms of support and went into a completely different area of business."

In short, Rosana had good reason to trust her instincts. When you see someone who takes risks and it works out time and time again, it's probably more than a coin-tossing contest. Life doesn't generally turn up heads so many times in a row. Good decision to leave Brazil. Good decision to get her PhD. And while Millennium didn't give her the ultimate promotion, it had set her on the path to real corporate responsibility.

Now she just needed to find a company that would recognize her potential by making her vice president of research. Renegade, a biotechnology company that ultimately became Aileron, seemed to check all the boxes.

All these years later, Rosana still speaks with excitement about the company's scientific possibility. "You take a peptide, a little protein, and you create a molecule that now can get into cells and modulate the ability of proteins to talk to each other. It's a major thing."

She pauses and, almost as if she were reliving the moment, switches to the present tense. "If this works, it [the technology] is really major. And so the science, the technology, was incredible. We had to prove it worked and develop the first product." Unfortunately, biotechnology companies don't just rely on science; they also need money and management.

"The problem was never the science. The problem was the management, the direction, and the leadership.

"I was so attracted by the fact that they were giving me the chance to be the VP of research and that they were going to put money in the company, I didn't care about anything else. I just didn't care. I said, 'This is my opportunity!'"

In her eagerness to get out of Millennium, receive the title she wanted, and pursue innovative science, Rosana didn't get help with the parts of the decision where she had less expertise. She could have reached out to friends who had experience conducting due diligence on biotechnology start-ups. In fairness, many people take jobs without sufficiently careful analysis. That decision alone did not feel like a huge mistake.

Unfortunately, like many venture-backed companies, money only trickled into the company and might not have come at all if Rosana hadn't devoted significant time to raising it herself. "I thought that was weird at the time, but I didn't really fully understand it, so I took it as it came. Then immediately, it became obvious to me that this company was not going to get off the ground unless we went outside and raised money from other investors. So we had to go out and raise a Series A [the first round of venture capital]." Not how she expected to spend her time as a scientist.

At an early strategy session to discuss how they could combine her company with another, the venture capitalist introduced her to a venture partner at their firm. He became her new boss.

"When I accepted the job and joined the company, this person was not there. So, I wasn't even given the chance to do that background."

"This person." Rosana has a hard time even mentioning his name.

It's rare to see a highly successful, highly confident person appear so flummoxed by the mere mention of a former boss. When she describes him, the reaction becomes more understandable. From the outset, Rosana found him troublingly aggressive and demeaning.

"He scared the hell out of us even at that first meeting. I remember walking out of that meeting and saying to my colleague, 'Do you want to work with him?' He looked at me, and we said, 'Yes, we want to do this.' We decided to do it together. We would protect each other. But it was not the right thing to do."

The boss seemed to revel in belittling the team. "He was the kind of person that would walk into our executive team meeting and say things like, 'You are all losers!'"

Rosana felt that he prioritized the wrong things, such as face time; couldn't make decisions; and then blamed others rather than owning problems.

"For example, in our business, we give contracts to outside organizations to get work done. He was so completely paranoid about the contracts that they would sit on his desk for three or six months. Then he would finally sign it, and then he would say, 'Where's the result of the experiment?'"

Even worse: "He was a gaslighter. We would say we couldn't do the experiment because you didn't sign the contract. And he said, 'This is not an excuse!'"

Rosana began to internalize his criticism and actually believe it. "I felt it was my fault. Then I would always try to do better . . . to basically meet his expectations, which were not possible to meet because" he hadn't articulated clear goals.

Rosana felt the impact acutely. "When I left Millennium, I thought I was on top of the world, that I knew everything. I didn't understand why they didn't give me the job."

After just a few months of working with her new boss, she experienced a complete change to her self-view. "I thought that not only you're not as good as you think you are, you're actually bad. . . . My self-confidence was down the drain. I was second-guessing myself on everything."

The impact extended into every aspect of her life. "I definitely was not smiling. I was not talking. I had three children. They were young, and I just basically couldn't take care of anyone. I was neglecting my children. I was neglecting my husband. I was neglecting the rest of the family. All I could do is basically manage myself, go to work, come back home."

Rosana knew from her medical training and personal experience that she had fallen into a deep psychological hole. "I had a bout of depression after my first child was born, so I knew how it felt." This time it was different.

Her daughter's bat mitzvah—where work so preoccupied Rosana that she could not fully experience joy—felt like "the breaking point," yet she didn't leave for another two years. All that time, the cost to her kept growing.

While Rosana easily identified the pain her decision caused and the regret she felt, she had a harder time identifying the reasons she had stayed. She had fleeting notions and conjectures, but unlike in her professional life, where she applied painstaking analysis and process to discover root causes, she relied on intuition. It was as if all the skills she'd learned examining the natural world had evaporated. She hoped that the answer would just occur to her.

We knew how she felt.

When we began the interviews, we too relied heavily on intuition. We often felt as if we had an answer based on some combination of experience and gut instinct. Having read Malcolm Gladwell's *Blink*, we knew that the unconscious mind can make highly accurate judgments in some situations. People do figure out some questions with a spontaneous reaction. The more we jumped to a conclusion, however, the more we felt that it foreclosed lines of inquiry and clouded our thinking.

We also tried applying Occam's razor: the rule that the simplest choice among various options is most likely the accurate one. Using that approach, we formulated alternative answers and chose the simplest one. Expanding the range of answers helped, but the process still felt rather inorganic; we tried too hard to identify "the" mistake rather than letting it emerge more naturally.

Nothing felt entirely natural until we reminded ourselves of *matryoshka*—the Russian nesting doll. As we unpacked our stories, it felt like opening up doll after doll to find another story lying beneath the surface. It became an obvious analogy that resonated even more as we read about psychiatry and psychology and learned about our schemas and their origins.

A couple of decades after the "invention" of the nesting dolls, Sigmund Freud wrote, "We are what we are because we have been what we have been."[1] Of course, just like dolls—the mother on the outside and the baby on the inside—but in Freud's account the innermost nesting doll is yourself. Neither nesting dolls nor Freud fit neatly into today's understanding of schemas, but they gave us a way to make sense of how our past influenced our behavior.

To find our schemas, we had to go backward in time—in some cases all the way to our childhood. Only by going slowly through layer after layer had the real source of the mistake emerged. Lifting and looking made revelation possible and added to the legitimacy of the conclusion. As we did it for each other, and ultimately for the people we interviewed, we tried to avoid the temptation to jump to *the* answer. That jump would have likely led to dead ends and also prevented the satisfaction of self-discovery.

We also tried to remember how Alison, whose training as a psychologist proved invaluable, had helped us understand our own mistakes. She never passed judgment on us. Her patient and thoughtful questioning and her gentle observations taught us how curiosity can drive understanding. Without her help, we could not have gone so deeply so quickly. She also helped us decipher our interviews and recognize patterns that we might otherwise have missed.

We found ourselves using the word "why" over and over. Why had

Michael made an impulsive decision? Why had Josh been so cavalier about what he wrote in his diary? Why would Rosana put up with such a terrible boss?

The word "why" rattled around in our heads until we remembered a technique Sakichi Toyoda, the founder of Toyota, had learned when working with engineers. In an effort to improve his company's efficiency and car quality, he had invented the technique of asking the "Five Whys." When confronted with a process bottleneck or quality problem, the technique encourages the team to ask "Why?" five times, until they have found the root cause. The process works because it requires teams to go backward and forward in time and look deeper and deeper into how they work together.

Decades after Toyoda formulated it, Eric Ries adapted it in his book *The Lean Startup*. Ries's book showed how what had helped make Toyota the world's largest automobile manufacturer could also help software engineers find the causes of their bugs and inefficiencies.

Here's a simplified example. Imagine a salesperson checks her company's database to find a customer's purchasing history. Her query comes back with no matches.

She's confused, as she works frequently with that customer. She calls her help desk and asks, "Why isn't my customer in the database?"

After a quick check, the help desk reports that a programming error in a recent software update led to the problem.

The help desk calls the engineering team to report the situation. The engineering leader asks her team, "Why did this update have an error?"

One of the team members volunteers, "It was my first time working on the database and I didn't understand how the searches work." At first blush, it appears that the team found the mistake quickly.

The leader reacts favorably: "Thanks for your honesty. Why didn't anyone do a quality check before we went live with the update?"

Another team member answers, "The quality-assurance lead was out that day and we didn't want to slow down the release."

Now the engineering leader sounds a little annoyed: "Why didn't you follow the policy that requires QA before release?"

"What policy?" someone asks.

Then, the fifth why—"Why don't all of you know the policy?" the lead asks.

Silence. Finally, someone gently reminds the leader that they had skipped the policy training because of an earlier fire drill when they had another coding error that they needed to fix.

The "real" problem emerges: last-minute crises had perpetually distracted the team from learning the processes needed for clean updates. The Five Whys had illuminated that what appeared like a small mistake by a new team member actually reflected a deeper problem.

We struggled to find a time-tested technique that keeps appearing again and again across art, psychology, and business. At the heart of our conversations, at the center of helping Rosana figure out what had happened with her terrible boss, lay a universal approach built on widespread application and acceptance.

Nineteenth-century nesting dolls, Freud's focus on the past, Toyoda's curiosity, and Ries's approach to software development all linked together. Each in their own way encouraged us to keep gently asking why. They formed the basis for so many of the conversations you'll find in this book.

And it was through this process that Rosana discovered what lay at the heart of her mistake.

How bad did the situation at home become for her? "I almost ended up in the hospital. It almost destroyed my home life, almost destroyed my marriage." Still, she couldn't leave the job. "All because I wanted to prove to myself that I could make it work."

The pain went on and on. When it got so bad that it couldn't get any worse, Rosana began to take the risks necessary to change the company or ultimately her relationship to it.

Rosana met with the venture capitalist in New York to explain her boss's deficiencies. He listened sympathetically before suggesting that she become the CEO.

She hesitated. "I'm a scientist! I can't just jump into being the CEO."

He reassured her emphatically and promised "a whole group of people to coach" her. They compromised on her becoming the interim CEO until they could find a permanent successor.

It was, she remembers, a "wonderful conversation." She got back on the train to Boston and immediately called her closest, and fellow long-suffering, colleague at Aileron to report the good news.

That call went well. Rather than stopping there, however, she then called another scientist from one of the companies with which Aileron had merged. She thought that he too shared her animosity toward their boss. While he may have, that didn't stop him from calling the boss to report what Rosana had done.

The boss called the venture capitalist. The venture capitalist back-tracked. The boss kept his job. By the time Rosana's train had pulled into Boston, the situation was even worse than when she had left. The venture capitalist even denied having made the offer to her. She now had two people who felt comfortable gaslighting her.

It didn't help that Rosana's husband didn't want her to leave her job. He unquestionably saw the impact on her, but also worried about their financial stability given their three children in private schools. He worked outside the home, "but the difference is that in biotech, I made much more money than him." Why did her financial situation feel particularly precarious?

Oh yes, by this time her family's media empire in Brazil had gone bankrupt. Like other companies in emerging markets, they had taken on dollar-denominated debt, so when the Brazilian real depreciated, they had no way to meet their obligations.

Her husband's fear still resonates. "He never said, 'I'm here for you.' Then when I told him the first time that I was going to resign, he implored me not to resign because we couldn't live with just his salary. He was petrified, petrified. He would not support me leaving the job. He never said, 'Leave, and we'll figure it out.'"

Finally, what caused Rosana to make the break had nothing to do with finances or scientific studies; it didn't relate to boardroom drama or power struggles. It came down to basic human decency.

"In one of my efforts to bring the company together, I had a summer party at my house to celebrate the closing of the Series B or something else. Everybody was very excited about it. Of course, they wanted the CEO to be at the party. He said he would come with his wife and daughter. He didn't show up. He didn't call. So on Monday, when I walked into the company, I said, 'What happened?' He said, 'Oh, I had more important things to do. I decided to come to work, to work on your performance review.'

"I thought, 'This guy is a complete lost cause.' The following week, I resigned." By skipping the summer party, the CEO had "hammered" on Rosana one too many times.

"I just said, 'I don't give a shit.' I did not even tell my husband. Then he had to be supportive, but I had to come up with the solution on how we were going to make ends meet, which I did brilliantly. I must say so."

Rosana had spent years of her life suffering under an abusive boss. She had stayed for lots of good reasons—commitment to the science and the team, personal financial concerns—but she nevertheless considers the decision to stay a terrible mistake. Her husband and she still fight about that period of their lives.

Before she could think about her career, however, she had to restore her mental health. "Quitting was a big weight lifted. I felt like a million bucks. I felt free. I felt like I should have done this two years ago. I didn't have to sacrifice my life and my children's lives and my relationship with my husband and my health because of this idiot."

She went on to have terrific success at Nimbus, where she helped design novel molecules that led to breakthrough discoveries and created enormous wealth for investors, colleagues, and herself.

Still, despite that success, the pain of Aileron lingers. She looks back with regret that she didn't do thoughtful diligence on the company.

The decision to join Aileron, however, while based on a skimpy review and a less than perfect understanding of her motivations, feels far less consequential than her decision to stay. "For me personally, the mistake was to stay as long as I stayed."

That may partly reflect one of her most admirable qualities. "I'm an optimist. I love people. I love life. I love a challenge. I never think anything is impossible." That goes right back to her schema about risk-taking.

She also clearly took deep pride in what the company had created, which made leaving all the harder.

"It was my baby. We started with a blank sheet of paper and a publication. We took the science further. We convinced people to invest in us." That's a form of sunk-cost fallacy—the tendency to keep investing in a project or idea even though the benefit we're likely to receive may be lower than the expected costs.

We've all done it: stayed in a relationship that we don't enjoy because we've already spent so much time getting to know the other person, or poured money into an old car that keeps breaking down because we've already spent so much on the earlier repairs.

Letting go of anything where we've made a huge effort does not come easily. Especially when it's something as important as a job focused on serious science.

That all makes sense, but there was something so bad about her boss's behavior and something so unusual about this incredibly smart, optimistic woman choosing to stay involved with him for so long, that the situation begs for another explanation. Why had she continued to work for such a terrible boss?

"He was absolutely abusive. Absolutely controlling."

The words Rosana used came out organically and emphatically. They clearly harkened back to some memory or recollection. In our conversations about her mistake, we asked whether Rosana had previously witnessed behavior like her boss's. Slowly, and then with an incredible rush, Rosana remembered behavior she had witnessed as a child in 1960s and '70s. It had all the hallmarks of what happened to her at work—even echoing the way she described her boss.

"I can tell you if you have been in an emotional Slavic family that words can really hurt. My father was a great father and a terrible husband. He was very, very controlling. My mother lost all her connections. My father separated her from everyone.

"The most important thing for my mom was my father. We were consequences of her relationship to my father, and everything was about my dad."

It took a toll on her mother. "She was a neglectful mother. She would forget us in school. We would be in the principal's office with the lady calling my mom saying, 'Oh, the girls are here. Are you coming to pick them up?'"

So much so that Rosana had to pick up many of her mother's responsibilities.

"My parents were both very alpha narcissists. When they fought, they would leave the house and leave me with all the kids. I had to go after my parents, sort it out, and say, 'Hey, you guys have to make peace.' So my whole life, I had to be sort of the parent of my parents.

"My younger sister says that I was her role model to be a mom."

Those responsibilities, plus her mother's negligence, naturally caused tension between mother and daughter.

"I had a father who pumped me up all the time and thought that I was the best thing in his life."

And her mother?

"I do think there is a little bit of the blame where, I thought, if my mother was smarter, thinner, faster, then my father wouldn't be fighting with her all the time"—a fairly common reaction from children in families with similar dynamics.

Her father's isolating her mother only made the family tighter, more insular. As a result, when Rosana talks about her decision to leave Brazil to go to the United States, she described herself as "abandoning" her family. She didn't realize that she uses that word.

"I didn't even notice that I said that. Oh, my God! Because I am the oldest of five, and everybody was always dependent on me, both my parents and my younger siblings. It was pretty heavy if you think about it. That you have to take care of everyone. So I think that's why I use the word 'abandoned.'"

In psychological terms, Rosana had experienced "parentification"—which happens when a child takes on the role of parent in the family, providing emotional support to the parents and other children as well as taking on age-inappropriate tasks such as handling family finances.

While parentification can cause serious psychological wounds that manifest themselves through depression and pattern repetition (e.g., parental neglect of one's own children), it can also foster excellent problem-solving skills, competence, and a propensity for personal growth.[2] You can see many of those things in Rosana, including her remarkable capacity to take on new challenges, evolve as a person, and navigate through hard situations. It's also hard to hear about how her work separated her temporarily from her family without thinking about echoes of her own childhood.

The responsibilities she assumed on behalf of her parents as a child did not end once she got to America. Following the bankruptcy of the family business, she had to help her parents financially. "Whoever has money helps each other."

All that familial background almost certainly influenced how she reacted to her situation at Aileron. Without even realizing it, she found herself in her mother's role: hurt by a domineering man, damaged in ways that isolated her from her family, doubting her self-worth. She couldn't recognize the situation since it fit so tightly with her schema about relationships between powerful men and women who are dependent on them. A schema that developed from watching her parents.

She is the first to acknowledge that she neglected her children while she tried to accommodate, then remove, then simply survive an abusive boss. Painful whispers of her parents' relationship decades earlier.

Two important points about domineering behavior: First, the ways it descends from generation to generation. Second, the extent to which it involves control. Rosana experienced both and, in particular, the deeply controlling behavior of an abusive boss.

She had to contend with those emotions while simultaneously confronting the financial pressure of supporting both her immediate and broader family in Brazil.

No wonder she had a hard time recognizing her schema about powerful, hurtful men. Rosana's drive, optimism, and risk tolerance may not have provided the space to understand how the dynamics she'd witnessed as a child shaped her adult experiences. She couldn't decode her boss's behavior as hugely problematic partly because it was so familiar to her. That's no excuse for what he did; just a recognition that when left unexamined, trauma echoes through our lives.

And hitting her father with her lunch box? For many years, Rosana believed that she had hit him for no apparent reason. Then years later, her father explained that she had done it to stop an argument between her parents—one of many that the relationship triggered.

8

The Big Year

I n July 2008, Angelina Jolie and Brad Pitt had twins and sold the photo rights of the babies for a reported $14 million. *The Guardian* summarized the situation perfectly: "The only other photos that 'would possibly come that close is Britney Spears giving birth to an alien.'"[1] Brangelina ruled the tabloids.

A few months before the birth, David Frankel met Pitt at the seventeenth-century villa the couple had rented near the village of Correns in Provence. At that point in his career, David had directed multiple movies including the megahit *The Devil Wears Prada*, worked with stars such as Sarah Jessica Parker and Meryl Streep, and had even won an Academy Award. Nothing, however, quite compared to meeting Pitt at that moment, in that setting.

David was in Europe to promote his new movie, *Marley & Me*. Movies follow strange gestation cycles, so before *Marley* had even hit the theaters, David had turned his attention to his next project. He wanted to make one movie, *The Big Year* (more on that later), but the studio wanted him to make another: *Moneyball*, based on Michael

Lewis's bestselling book about Billy Beane, the Oakland Athletics' analytically driven general manager.

Amy Pascal, yes, the same woman who was Michael's partner during the Sony hack, had gone through three or four drafts of *Moneyball* when she asked David to work on it. After David read the drafts and the book, he could tell that the screenwriters hadn't cracked it. His children loved *Major League*, a great baseball movie, so he wanted to make something in that vein but base it on the *Moneyball* story.

David went to work with the writer of the original draft, who, in Hollywood terms, was a "nobody": someone who had no sway with the studio honchos. A year later, when they delivered it to Pascal, she said, "Great. I want to make it. But the only person I want to make it with is Brad Pitt."

If you don't work in Hollywood, this whole process will seem a bit bizarre, so take a deep breath. Michael Lewis wrote a great book. Sony optioned it. A bunch of writers drafted screenplays. David rewrote it with one of the original writers (who got fired and then rehired). Pascal liked their draft but wanted Pitt.

In movie terms, the action cuts to a beautiful courtyard next to a winery in Provence. Based on Amy's introduction, Pitt and David met to talk through David's draft. No screenwriter could have written the scene with a straight face: a helicopter sat on a tightly manicured lawn waiting to transport Angelina Jolie to the hospital, a majestic tree cast a soft shadow over the chairs, a silent staff member had laid out a beautiful charcuterie plate and a bottle of wine.

After preliminaries about friends in common and the standard exchange of professional praise, Pitt said, "I'd like to do the movie. I love the story, but I want to do the book. I don't want all the added drama."

Basically, it was a question of whether he wanted David's version—which made it a bit more dramatic—or one that stuck closely to the book.

It felt like a good conversation: two professionals who wanted to work together trying to see if they could find common ground. That made sense because before David went into the meeting, the studio had told him that Pitt was open-minded and eager to get David's thoughts.

The meeting ended inconclusively, but shortly thereafter Pitt demanded a different writer. So, in typical style, the studio hired the highest-priced, most successful writer in Hollywood—a guy named Steve Zaillian—to rewrite the script for Pitt. It didn't hurt that Zaillian had gone to high school with Pascal.

Fast-forward a few months. Zaillian finished his rewrite; Pitt liked it; the studio liked it (probably because Pitt liked it); and then there's David. What to do about him? Pitt had made clear he preferred Zaillian's version, but Amy still wanted David to direct and hoped that David and Pitt could resolve their differences. David still preferred his draft but was intrigued since Amy suggested that Pitt had an open mind.

When in doubt, have a meeting. David and Pitt got together at a Los Angeles coffee shop to once again exchange pleasantries, discuss scripts, and size up the idea of working together.

Again, the meeting ended inconclusively. David caught the red-eye back to Miami to rejoin his family. That afternoon, while on the golf course, in the midst of a round that undoubtedly suffered from the poor sleep he'd had on the plane, David received an email from Pitt: "If you're going to direct it, I don't want to do it. We just have different visions for it."

Basically a polite way of saying: I win, you lose—since Pitt knew that the studio would only make the movie with him and he knew that David was, well, like the original screenwriter, dispensable.

Having traveled to Provence to meet Pitt at his Brangelina fairyland, suffered through the indignity of having Zaillian rewrite his script, and then indulged in another Hollywood Kabuki meeting at the coffee shop, David felt that the whole thing had been some kind of pro forma bullshit.

Pitt's fast response suggested that he hadn't had an open mind at the meeting the day before. David was angry at the studio for asking him to meet again, angry at himself for letting Pitt seduce him into thinking that Pitt cared about what David thought, and angry at Pitt for being so damn charming.

David immediately forwarded the email to Rosalie, his manager: "He's obviously not as good an actor as he thinks he is because I saw right through him every step of the way." Which, of course, David hadn't.

Here's the thing: David had not hit Forward; he had hit Reply. Within eight seconds, he got an email back from Pitt: "What the fuck, buddy?!"

At a moment when his career had just taken off, David had told the biggest star in the world, who was married to the other biggest star—a couple with $14 million babies—that he was a phony. David was mortified. He never intended to insult Pitt.

You don't have to work in Hollywood to know that fucking with Brangelina was a mistake. A really big mistake with two causes. First, David hadn't considered his emotional state when he hit Reply instead of Forward. A moment of anger led to a lack of focus, which resulted in sending the email to the wrong address. A high-stakes version of a mistake so many people make.

He also hadn't had particularly good situational awareness. From the middle of a jet-lagged round of golf probably isn't the best place to manage your career.

Here's the surprising part: When we asked David to tell us about a mistake he regretted, he didn't choose this story. He only mentioned it in passing as a diverting anecdote. As it turned out, David admired the finished version of *Moneyball*, written by Steve Zaillian and directed by Bennett Miller, and particularly enjoyed the Oscar-nominated performance by Pitt.

Pissing off Pitt hadn't proven emotionally or professionally costly.

Instead, David wanted to talk about how he persuaded a major movie studio to make *The Big Year*, a movie filmed at locations around the world with an all-star cast that included Steve Martin, Owen Wilson, and Jack Black. A movie that cost $45 million to make and grossed $8 million in theaters. A bomb and a half. The kind of move that can cost people their careers. In short, David had bet his entire career on a movie about bird-watching.

To understand David's mistake, it helps to go back to Germany during the 1930s. As a young Jewish student, David's father, Max, had to sit in the hall while the other students sang Nazi songs. From his earliest memories, he was the "other." His family fled to the United States shortly before the Holocaust and arrived knowing no English. Throughout Max's long, illustrious career—one that culminated in becoming executive editor of *The New York Times*—he combined a journalist's detachment with a refugee's sense of being the outsider.

He assimilated by learning the language—both the syntax and the idioms—and by supporting the Yankees, but Max also insisted that journalists needed to avoid even the appearance of bias or preference. David's parents didn't join causes or make commitments outside work. So much so that David's father even resented joining a neighborhood club in Chevy Chase, Maryland, where his children could swim and play tennis. For Max Frankel, "joining" meant Nazi Youth parades down the avenues of Weissenfels, Germany, which led to persecution and exile.

David's childhood, in a home filled with intellectual curiosity, distinguished visitors, and parents who "mattered" in Washington and New York, contrasted sharply with his father's, but the family still maintained their role as observers rather than full participants in the world they helped shape.

Just as Max had done his best to assimilate, David worked hard to fulfill his immigrant father's definition of success: great student, excellent athlete, and, perhaps best of all, admission to Harvard. David arrived at Harvard just as it had begun to admit a more egalitarian, diverse student body. Prep school students from Andover, St. Paul's, Groton, and Exeter still made up a huge percentage of the class; it was not unusual to come across fourth-generation students whose family names adorned the buildings and professorships.

Yet, those students now shared dorms with a smattering of first-generation Harvard students who carried the expectations of their families alongside their own ambitions. David observed the legacy students and wanted no part of their world. Instead, he spent his time playing tennis, a sport at which he excelled and where all that mattered was his own performance. He loved the simple honesty of the tennis ladder: you played on a team, but each week you competed against your own teammates for your spot.

Socially, it did not even occur to him to try to join Harvard's most exclusive social organizations: the Final Clubs. Created as a haven for the sons of proper families, clubs such as the Porcellian had welcomed Teddy Roosevelt, Oliver Wendell Holmes (father and son), and Henry Cabot Lodge. Given the era, and the lingering prejudice toward the growing number of Jews on campus, it was by no means clear that these clubs would have wanted David regardless of his interest. While not quite Joseph in Egypt, he was a stranger in a strange land.

So, David and his roommates created the Luge Club, an imaginary organization formed to mock the Final Clubs. The Luge Club had its own faux traditions and hosted dinners where the members applied their dry, outsider humor to a culture that seemed as foreign to the members as they would have seemed to the WASPs who dominated parts of the college.

Yet David had also clearly wanted to attend Harvard—an institution filled with "insider" traditions. He created at Harvard what he had witnessed at home: a seat inside the tent, but on a chair pulled to the side of the ring. A seat where he could watch the circus with detachment while still participating when so inclined. He focused on activities where he knew that his success was of his own making, not the product of his pedigree—each week fighting his way up or falling down the tennis ladder. Starting at an early age, David preferred activities—such as tennis—that didn't depend on the approval or acquiescence of others.

He developed a strongly held schema about the importance of proving himself without the help of others and avoiding the temptation to pay too close attention to what others thought.

That schema got reinforced during his first exposure to Hollywood. The summer after his sophomore year, a family friend introduced him to Robert Evans, the legendary producer, who made iconic movies such as *The Godfather* and *Love Story*. David drove out to LA hoping to have Evans get him a job as a production assistant on a movie set.

He went into Evans's Mussolini-like office at Paramount. Surrounded by all the trappings of an imperial executive, Evans skipped the pleasantries: "What do you want to do?"

"I want to be a writer."

"Then why do you want to be a production assistant on a set? What do you think you're going to do?"

"I don't know, I'll be on the set. I'll see how movies are made."

Evans shouted back at him, "No, you won't! You won't see anything about how movies are made. You'll just get coffee for people. What are you going to learn from that? You want to be a writer? Go home and write."

To his credit, David did exactly what Evans proposed. After college and a brief sojourn on the corporate side of the movie business in Los Angeles and New York, he quit and moved to Miami, a city with virtually no production infrastructure and with a wildly different culture from Hollywood's.

Why Miami? Well, Jennifer, who later became his wife, ran an advertising agency in Miami and had given David the choice of living in

Miami or finding a new girlfriend. His rationale extended beyond his commitment to Jen. While working at his corporate job, David had seen how deals got done in Hollywood: the long lunches, intense networking, and mutual back-scratching.

It reminded him of the Washington he'd witnessed at family dinner parties and of Harvard's clubbiness—without the patrician veneer. Miami allowed him to court Jen, get to work writing, and avoid any temptation to join the insider entertainment game.

By living in Miami, he didn't get defined by seating charts at popular restaurants or invitations to exclusive parties. He didn't want to know who was up or down and definitely didn't want others thinking about him in those same terms. David set to work on shows that he would want to watch.

He even wrote several of them while living in Los Angeles before he moved to Miami. First came forty episodes of *Doctor Doctor*. Then, in 1991, he wrote the pilot for *Grapevine*, which ultimately got picked up by CBS after generating lots of buzz.

Notwithstanding his writing productivity in LA, he felt liberated in Miami—freed from the intermingling of social and professional commitments, unbound from the norms that drove success for other writers and directors.

Suddenly—in Hollywood terms that meant after almost ten years of effort—David was a "successful" comedy writer. Back in those days, this kind of success meant that the studios came calling with a "development deal." In David's words, "a whole shitload of money—millions of dollars—guaranteed for three years—all for somebody in their twenties." David turned the offers down because he didn't want to get trapped in a corporate setting.

Peter Chernin, a highly successful CEO of Fox, even offered David thirteen episodes guaranteed to air, a deal Chernin had never offered anyone before. David listened to the offer and turned it down on the spot. His agent, Nancy Josephson, just about levitated off her chair when David said no.

David just didn't want to feel beholden to anyone or risk that he'd have to adjust what he did out of a sense of obligation to Chernin. Chernin listened to David's reasoning and replied, "Thank you for talking me out of that offer. I will never offer it to anyone else." Nancy looked as if she were going to cry.

Around the same time, Jeffrey Katzenberg, who ran Disney's studio, saw *Grapevine* and became interested in working with David. Attracting Katzenberg's interest was for David a bit like the creative director at an award-winning, avant-garde regional-theater company getting asked to produce and direct a Broadway show.

Nancy said that he should fly out to Los Angeles to meet Katzenberg. David declined, saying, "You know, they make crappy movies. I'm flattered, but he's going to offer me some crappy movie and I'm going to have to say no."

Once again, Nancy listened as her client tried to club his career to death. Clearly shocked that he wouldn't jump at the opportunity, she tried to reason with him: "No, he just wants to meet with you."

David didn't buy it. "What are we going to talk about? One of those superficial Hollywood meetings? 'I like your work.' 'Oh, thank you, and I like your work too.' We have nothing to talk about. When we have something to talk about, I'll meet with him."

Finally, after six months, David agreed to meet with Katzenberg.

The conversation unfolded much as David had predicted: "I love your work" and "I love yours too." When they got around to talking about a deal, David declined what Katzenberg offered and proposed an alternative:

"You know what? I'm going to go write a movie on spec. And I promise you, because of all your calling, I'll let you read it first."

Six months later, David sent the screenplay of *Miami Rhapsody* to

Katzenberg. Within a day or two, Katzenberg called David: "Okay, let's make it." Not just that, but Katzenberg agreed to David's request for how to make it.

David told him, "I want to make the lowest-budget movie you ever made at Disney, and I want to make it in Miami." And David did. They made *Miami Rhapsody* for $5 million—with an all-star cast: Mia Farrow, Antonio Banderas, Sarah Jessica Parker, and Naomi Campbell.

In short, David's film-directing career began only because he had turned down Chernin and played incredibly hard to get with Katzenberg. David declined the development deals that studios offered, passed on the golden ticket into the Disney empire, and, instead, took the risk of writing his own movie with no guarantee of ever getting it made.

It might not have been a straight line from the Luge Club to *Miami Rhapsody*, but in the movie version of David's life you'd hear Frank Sinatra singing "My Way" as Katzenberg green-lights David's movie.

Following *Miami Rhapsody*, David wrote and directed the pilot for *Dear Diary*, an unusually formatted show driven primarily by narration. As a television series, it had virtually no chance of success, but the pilot generated such enthusiasm that DreamWorks distributed it through theaters so that it could qualify for an Academy Award. Less than three months later, David got called to the stage of the Dorothy Chandler Pavilion to collect the first (and only) Oscar for Best Short ever awarded to a television sitcom pilot. It was the ultimate insider prize for outsider art.

David's career really took off. He directed fabulous TV shows (*Band of Brothers* and *Sex and the City*), made incredibly successful movies (*The Devil Wears Prada*), and did it all while still living in Miami, staying married, and helping to raise two children.

It's worth pausing to describe *Devil's* success: the movie cost $35 million to make, grossed $325 million at the box office, and won two Academy Award nominations, including one for Meryl Streep as Best

Actress in a Leading Role. Even today, it's hard to get on a plane or turn on cable television without seeing it.

With David's growing success, the studios sent him scripts and story ideas, pitched his agent on projects, and generally showered him with the kind of attention that they reserved for proven moneymakers. One idea kept coming back: *Marley & Me*. David had turned the script down several times, which forced the studio to have someone else do a rewrite and go into preproduction with another director.

That didn't go well, which led the studio to seek David's help, again. David had a plan: "My sole goal was to make a movie that made people cry as much as *Love Story*. That was my mantra. To just wreck people." He fixed the script, made a very successful movie, and, importantly for this story, really endeared himself to the studio executives while maintaining his outsider persona. Mission accomplished.

He was hot. The executives with whom he was closest, both at Fox, loved him and expressed it in Hollywood terms: "Whatever you want to do, we want to do."

But did they really mean it? And how could David decipher what they said since he was working in Hollywood and not living in it? He had high enthusiasm for films and meaningful detachment from the community that made them.

The skepticism about belonging that he had learned from his father and had practiced at Harvard carried into his professional life. He cared much more about his work than what other people thought of it. Contrast that to most Hollywood professionals, who had high "public self-consciousness"—their sense of self depended meaningfully on how others perceived them.

In 1995, Mark Leary and his colleagues developed sociometer theory, which argues that our self-esteem serves as a barometer of social inclusion and rejection. Unsurprisingly, people who feel accepted and appreciated usually have high self-esteem; conversely, rejection and disdain damage their sense of self.[2] In extreme cases, social rejection is a predictor of all sorts of bad outcomes from anger and aggressive behavior to suicide.

The desire for social acceptance can leak into work contexts, as evidenced by how it influenced Michael's decision to green-light *The Interview*. Even people who don't feel the need for acceptance, however, may seek another form of approval: status. While psychologists use sociometer theory to help explain how the desire for positive self-esteem drives behaviors that lead to social *inclusion*, hierometer theory posits that self-esteem is also a barometer of social *status* (e.g., social rank, level of prestige and influence). To maintain self-esteem, we seek not just acceptance but also status.[3]

We've all seen manifestations of both behaviors in work and social settings. Some people try too hard to appease their colleagues and friends; other people manifest a desire for status by speaking too much in meetings or demanding to make all the plans for a night out.

There's actually a third approach to group dynamics that relates closely to David's experience. He knew he needed the support of studio executives to do the work he loved, but he constantly evaluated himself and his work based on his intrinsic values rather than his sociometer or hierometer "score." He prioritized what psychologists call private self-consciousness. People with a high degree of private self-consciousness generally stick to their own true north; they have a lower tendency to conform when others challenge their opinions.[4]

Public and private self-consciousness can lead to very different behaviors. People who over-index to public self-consciousness risk having their desire for likability and acceptance distort their decisions. People who only follow their own true north sometimes do not adjust to important professional and interpersonal dynamics.

David's true north actually kept him due south: in Miami. He was neither a studio insider nor a true outsider. We think of him as the "stranger." So many movies have a similar character: the man who arrives in town and sees its inhabitants and mores with a cool, distant perspective.

The expression also conjures up a famous piece of European writing. And, no, we don't mean Camus's classic existentialist novel. In 1908, Georg Simmel, one of the founders of modern sociology, wrote an essay titled "The Stranger." He described the role of people who join societies of which they are not original members. That vantage point enhances their ability to avoid the biases encouraged by local norms. Simmel also observed how it may keep them distant from the center of power. The concept must have resonated personally for Simmel, who, as a Jew, joined Germany's institutions of higher learning but never became fully accepted by them.

Max Frankel's experience in the United States echoes Simmel's. Max achieved extraordinary success at *The New York Times*, an institution that embodied the Northeastern establishment, but always—through choice and necessity—separated himself from the communities he covered as a journalist and editor. Simmel wrote, "The stranger is not radically committed to the unique ingredients and peculiar tendencies of the group, and therefore approaches them with the specific attitude of 'objectivity.'"[5]

Father and son fit squarely into that mold. For Max Frankel, it propelled his career. For David, it helped provide the creativity and perspective that made his work compelling. It also reinforced his tendency to prioritize his own values at any cost.

Having had great success with *The Devil Wears Prada* and *Marley & Me*, David had three choices.

Option 1: He could parlay this success into the opportunity to direct a big-budget franchise movie (e.g., something like a Marvel movie) or start his own production company.

Ryan Coogler made *Creed* and *Fruitvale Station*, then directed

Black Panther. Chloé Zhao directed *Nomadland* and followed up by directing the star-studded Marvel franchise *Eternals.* Nothing says "welcome to the club" like having a studio trust you with their most valuable franchise.

Option 2: He could go back to writing and directing small-budget, quirky television shows and movies.

Option 3: He could take the studio executives at face value when they said, "Whatever you want to do, we want to do."

Often, in complicated situations, we hear what we want to hear. When David heard the studio's encouragement, he thought they had truly granted him the autonomy he felt that he had earned. He didn't understand that most directors chose Option 1 for a reason: that's what studios want because it aligns their best talent with their most valuable properties.

How did David decide? Compare, for a moment, his career to a poker game. At no point had he drawn great cards (he had had to write or rewrite all his scripts rather than get handed a script that the studio wanted to make), but through a willingness to bluff, fold, and go all in at the right moments (all the discussions with Katzenberg), he'd won round after round (made the movies he wanted to make).

With that background, it's therefore unsurprising that David chose Option 3, which brings us to *The Big Year* and the biggest mistake of David's career.

In movie terms, we've come to the end of Act I—the whole period before he made his mistake. A highly successful writer and director is flying high. Would that success propel him to even greater heights or set him up for a fall?

It's important to remember that the decision came at a moment of peak self-confidence, and high self-confidence increases our willingness to take big risks. Even more than that, it goes back to David's orientation toward private self-consciousness, following his internal guides versus going along to get along. In some ways, David's decision to make *The Big Year* reflected his focus on respect over acceptance. He'd acted outside the Hollywood tribe, had gained the respect of the tribe, and now felt self-confident about making his own decision.

Independence, original thinking, and an outsider's perspective all carry positive connotations. They work best, however, when applied in a knowing, self-aware manner that relates to their context. When David had heard the studio executives offer Option 3, he thought that they actually meant it. They didn't.

Despite all his experience, David didn't realize the extent to which studio executives spoke a different language and played the game by different rules. It turns out that effective ways to learn group norms as an adult resemble what works on grammar school playgrounds.

Ken Dodge, a psychologist and professor at Duke University, and his colleagues did a classic study of elementary school boys to find out what strategies most successfully allowed newcomers to join a peer group playing together. They found that the advice we all got as children —"Just ask to join!"—is not the most successful approach. Students had more success joining the group if they first observed it in order to learn the dynamics and rules, then mimicked the group, and finally approached by saying something positive about the activity (e.g., "That looks like a fun game"). Importantly, children who enter groups the most successfully try to fit into the group by following the group's rules and norms rather than disrupting, seeking attention, or doing things "their" way.[6]

Compare that to David's experience with Hollywood. While David had done an amazing job observing from afar, his distance had made him less attuned to the nuances that prevent mistakes and then help people overcome them. He watched, but never really wanted to join the game.

Few people close to David or at the studios understood the appeal of the movie David wanted to make, and virtually no one liked his decision.

In 2004, Mark Obmascik published *The Big Year*, a book about how three men competed to see who could spot the most varieties of birds in North America in one year. Obmascik is a serious, Pulitzer Prize–winning journalist, and outdoor fanatics generally loved the book.

It's also a book about bird-watching. Not baseball. Not Wall Street or Washington political scandals. There's no sex—except for mating calls. No car chases or catwalks. While many people bird-watch, virtually no one who doesn't is interested in the topic. It's sort of like travel mishaps: when they happen to you, they seem important and kind of incredible; when you tell others about them, your audience tunes them out.

David had had great success taking a niche field—fashion magazines—and making a bestseller accessible to an even bigger audience. That's partly because fashion is highly marketable. It's much harder if you start with a topic that revolves around men sitting on frozen tundra trying to spot a thimble-sized thrush.

There are lots of hard movies to make. One of the hardest is taking an obscure subject, often based on a nonfiction book, and turning it into a compelling movie. David thought, "So many of the projects in Hollywood that we admire are the ones where people fought to get something done that no one else wanted to do and then [it] turned out to be a big success. This will be mine." What made him want to do it?

Partly, he knew that Jen had grown up bird-watching with her father. Perhaps he also saw himself in the story: characters who did something that no one else understood, characters who played their own game regardless of how others perceived it. Movies that are meant to please your wife or help you examine your life journey, however, shouldn't feature big comedic stars and cost $45 million.

David had good reason to feel confident. Just like *The Big Year*, *The Devil Wears Prada* was based on a book, and the script for that blockbuster success hadn't come easily. After David read an early draft of *Devil*, Rosalie, his manager, had asked him to get on the phone with the producer, Wendy Finerman. David agreed, but then two hours before the call he reread the script and realized, "Oh, God. I can't direct a single scene in this script. This is not a good script. I don't believe in one moment of it."

So, David called Rosalie to say, "Tell her I have a childcare emergency; I can't deal with this." The meeting got postponed, and then a week later, Finerman asked again to have the call.

David remembers this moment clearly. Rosalie called to ask, "When do you want this meeting?"

"Did you read the script? It's terrible."

And Rosalie almost yelled at David. "What do you think? Do you think that they're sending you a Shakespearean finished product? What do you think your job is? You're David Frankel! You think that Spielberg gets finished scripts perfectly ready to shoot?"

David learned from reworking *Devil* that he could shape the story even when starting with suboptimal material—as long as it contained the kernel of a compelling story. He had done it once and thought he could do it again.

In Hollywood, the only thing worse than making a bad movie is missing the chance to make a successful one. On the one hand, no one really wanted to make *The Big Year*; on the other, no one wanted to risk *not* participating in another Frankel blockbuster. So a bidding war unfolded over a movie that the studios didn't even really want to make. At the end, Tom Rothman, a powerful studio executive, won out, but with the proviso that, due to a series of bizarre contractual commitments, the movie had to cost at least $45 million to make. The budget had a floor, not a ceiling. On a movie that Rothman didn't even really want David to make.

That David couldn't spend *less* than $45 million meant that he couldn't make a low-budget, quirky film like the one that had launched his career. The difficult process of getting the film made, including

Rothman's lack of enthusiasm, only increased David's enthusiasm. He liked swimming against the stream and wanted to prove people wrong.

They cast famous stars such as Steve Martin and Owen Wilson and built out a long filming schedule, which included shooting in Vancouver, the Yukon, Joshua Tree National Park, Times Square, and the Florida Keys. The filmmakers went everywhere and tried everything, eventually spending every penny of the $45 million for a movie that could have cost half as much.

While $45 million sounds like a big budget, it's actually neither a low-budget indie nor a big-budget blockbuster. *The Big Year* was caught in the middle: a big enough budget that the studio cared, but not so big that they really needed it to succeed. They had backed a director they trusted and wanted to make happy, but not someone with whom they had a long-term deal.

David wanted to make people laugh and cry; he wanted to use the budget and freedom that he had earned with Hollywood *insiders* to make an *outsider* movie. To use a tennis analogy, he found himself caught midcourt, neither rushing the net nor hitting from the baseline. It's the most vulnerable position in tennis, and in a career.

When they finished filming, Rothman watched the movie and called David with his comments. It was a civil, polite call, and ninety minutes long. For minute after endless minute Rothman told David everything that he disliked about the movie and everything that they should have done differently. David took twenty pages of notes. At the end of the call, David realized that even the most hopelessly devoted employee could not execute all the changes Rothman wanted in the movie.

That version of the movie just didn't exist.

Rothman clearly hated it. So much so that he hired a completely separate editing team to make a version that David didn't get to see until they had finished. That never happens in Hollywood or, if it does, only in highly antagonistic situations where a movie is way over budget or badly delayed.

Now there were two versions of a movie that had an artificially inflated budget: one by David, the other under the auspices of the studio head who didn't support the project from the outset.

David had good reason to trust his own instincts. When he'd finished editing *Miami Rhapsody*, Katzenberg wanted to rename the movie *Can't Buy Me Love*, after the hit song. David said, "'No.' Two months later Katzenberg was fired and we kept the name I wanted."

When he made *The Devil Wears Prada*, Rothman felt unenthusiastic about Anne Hathaway for lead, but David had fought for her. The audience loved her.

When the studio screened *The Devil Wears Prada*, Rothman said, "That only went pretty well. I think you're going to get a score in the high seventies [movies get tested with audiences that rate them on a score of 1 to 100]. Here are my notes." He gave David a "buck" slip with about twenty-five different scribbled notes on the front and back. Rothman said, "I think if you do these, you'll raise your score. But if you get anything above an eighty-five, you don't have to do these." The movie scored about an 88, so they didn't use a single one of Rothman's notes.

When *Devil* became a huge hit, David felt, in his own words, that the scoreboard read FRANKEL 2, ROTHMAN 0. Then on *Marley*, David largely ignored Rothman's advice, including deciding to cast Alan Arkin in a major role over Rothman's objection. They also fought about the end of the movie. Rothman was adamant that the family should get a new dog after Marley died, while David felt equally strongly that they should not. As a compromise, David agreed to show flashbacks, but stood firm on the overall ending. Again, the movie performed well, so David felt that he had gone 3–0. The whole experience read more as a tennis match than a team sport.

When Rothman then said he liked his cut of *The Big Year* better than David's, David demanded that the studio test them both simultaneously with similar audiences. The studio agreed that the winner would get released. David's version won, but there's no winning in Hollywood if you piss off your boss. That it always remained civil in no way diminished the intensity of the disagreement.

There's another way to think about the dynamic. We're all motivated by self-interest: the desire to get what we want. Yet concern for others—the way we cooperate with colleagues—eventually drives much of our success and happiness. Directors don't get hired and rehired unless they have strong "other concern"; they have to work with high-powered and often-temperamental movie stars and studio executives.

David took the studio's decision to give him $45 million for *The Big Year* as support for the project without recognizing that it was actually just support for him. He didn't make the studio his partner; he didn't get them emotionally invested in the project.

Rothman released David's version as promised—with one cruel twist. *The Devil Wears Prada* got released in about three thousand theaters and *Marley* in around twenty-five hundred theaters. *The Big Year* opened in about two hundred theaters. There was no advertising. There was no marketing. Zero. The movie sank without a trace. With all of the $45 million spent, it grossed less than $8 million.

Act II closed with *The Big Year* bombing at the box office. Notwithstanding this painful conclusion, David didn't immediately recognize the impact on his decision-making or career.

Right after *The Big Year*, David chose to make *Hope Springs* because it gave him the chance to work with Meryl Streep, along with Tommy Lee Jones and Steve Carell. Again, David chose a less than obvious storyline—an older couple solving their sexual problems. The movie, while not a huge hit, did find an audience—and profitability.

That success, and the satisfaction David took from operating with a wider degree of freedom, led him to work next with Harvey Weinstein, on a movie called *One Chance*, the story of a young opera singer. David made that choice despite warnings from virtually everyone he trusted that working with Weinstein could only end in tears. In some sense, the warnings only reinforced Weinstein's appeal. David wanted to work with him because David believed that "[Weinstein] was working outside the system; he didn't respect the rules; he completely appreciated passion and recognized talent."

Early on in that project, David felt that he had made the right choice as he "won" all his encounters with Weinstein—a rare feat for anyone who worked with the Weinstein Company. David quickly realized, however, that working with Weinstein always became unrelentingly painful. They ultimately fought about everything, from the music to the edits.

It got so bad that David called his agent to say, "I want off this movie. I want to leave." A combination of his sense of duty and his agent's persuasiveness kept him on the job, but unsurprisingly, all that confrontation had come at a cost. Weinstein, like Rothman, controlled the marketing and the distribution.

Weinstein buried *One Chance*. David ended up suing Harvey Weinstein for not fulfilling his commitments and wonders to this day if that decision, which led to corrosive, expensive litigation (is there any other kind?), might have reflected the resentment he unconsciously harbored over what had happened on *The Big Year*.

After *The Big Year* mistake, David hadn't given himself the time or permission to process what had happened and, as a result, made a version of the same mistake again. So much of what went wrong on both—ignoring advice, trying to make an obscure subject relatable—reflected the complexity of David's desire to simultaneously participate in the game while still maintaining his distance.

When you make a bad career mistake because you don't understand your environment or because you're overconfident, it stings. When you compound it by doing it again, that really hurts. David regrets it in two ways.

From an early age, David played individual competitive sports—sports where you had to compete for your position every week. Even the best golfers and tennis players operate with no reservoir of goodwill; you're judged on your most recent match.

Until he made *The Big Year*, David had applied the same principle to his career. In his vernacular, he hadn't "cashed any checks" from his previous success; he thought, "Everyone's work should just speak for itself." Sure, Katzenberg wanted to work with David, but the *Miami Rhapsody* screenplay sold itself. He had to sell the studios on his versions of *Devil* and *Marley*. It was like the tennis ladder: he had to compete anew every day.

Tony Soprano famously said to his team, "'Remember when' is the lowest form of conversation." David never wanted to be the guy who had to refer back to his older work to secure his next assignment. He wanted his work, not his track record, to determine his success.

He has a hard time distinguishing between the credibility he earned through his work and the kind of privilege he dislikes. It felt especially painful to take advantage of something he generally mistrusted—insider status—only to have it fail. If you compromise a core value, the mistake can linger for years. Especially when that compromise also hurts your career.

It went right back to his father. From an early age, David had a faint thought rattling in his brain: "If I join a club, does that make me a Nazi?" That thought stayed with him even into adulthood. Of course, he recognizes the limitation of the comparison. "I feel like our experiences are so profoundly different that I feel awkward making that connection. I feel like where it's accurate is that while I'm obviously not a journalist, I kept the journalist's sensibility of noncommitment."

He kept the "noncommitment" to Hollywood culture, but never lost his competitive instincts. Like athletes who have better and worse games and seasons, movie directors have flops and hits. Even Steven Spielberg made clunkers, and great movies came from "one-hit" directors. No one is as good or as bad as their best or worst work.

That pattern, that sine curve of highs and lows, requires a complex kind of acceptance. Behind David's subtly charming, modest demeanor lies a competitiveness that has helped him excel across so many aspects of his life. Perhaps *The Big Year* has stayed with David because it represented his first meaningful failure, and it represents the reality that not every movie can attain *Devil's* success. Note the use of the word "failure." A group of people came together to work on a serious project that didn't have commercial success. That's quite different from the mistake David made in choosing to make *The Big Year*.

For the first time in his career, David felt a different kind of fear after *The Big Year*. As he puts it, "Part of trying to break the mold is really fear of failure. If you don't do what everyone else is doing, then you're not compared to everyone else. So you can't fail on the more popular definition of success."

Ironically, the success of *Devil* changed the way the industry judged him. Commercial success became the standard, so *The Big Year*'s disappointing results jeopardized his ability to keep working in the field that he adored. He needed another big hit to become a bankable director. While the movie didn't close the door, David knows that it had an impact. "I went from making big movies to making smaller movies. And now many years later I have to fight to justify my salary."

For all the pain that the movie caused, David holds no grudges, partly because studios continue to want him to direct their most bankable actors such as Will Smith, Edward Norton, and Helen Mirren on *Collateral Beauty*, and Bryan Cranston and Annette Bening on *Jerry & Marge Go Large*. Even as we wrote, David had begun shooting the sequel to *The Devil Wears Prada*, with the original cast.

He holds no one accountable other than himself. He even has a certain empathy for the way studio heads must assemble complex teams and gamble millions of dollars on projects that have no certainty of success. While Rothman and David are not friends, they've stayed in touch.

In the end, the most satisfying moment of the process came on a relatively small screen in a drab editing facility around the corner from his father-in-law's house in Miami. His mother-in-law had just died; his wife was mourning; his father-in-law suddenly needed to use a wheelchair.

They wheeled his father-in-law into the cutting room to show him *The Big Year*. He could barely sit through the whole thing. At the end of the movie, he wept. Jen said that she loved it. Then David's father came to see it and he too loved it. When David showed it to Elizabeth Gabler, with whom he had made *Devil* and *Marley* when she worked at Fox, she grabbed his arm and said, "This is your best movie yet."

David thinks, "It's a very sweet movie. I'm very proud of it. It's quite a beautiful movie actually." Only an outsider could keep that kind of perspective about a movie that almost ruined his career.

9

Traffic Stop

On Christmas Day 2013, Karol Mason sat in the kitchen of her Atlanta home. The sweet smells of the holiday blanketed the room: Cornish game hens, collard greens, macaroni and cheese, and desserts—lots and lots of desserts. Most years, Karol's family crowded into the kitchen jostling and joking in anticipation of the celebration.

Since she had bought the house, roughly ten years earlier, it had become, by virtue of its size and quiet suburban neighborhood, a gathering place. The home's newness, the area's large lots, and the tall pines that guarded the community's privacy spoke to Karol's professional success.

That year, unlike the previous boisterous celebrations, the family sat silently checking their phones and staring at the door that separated the kitchen and the garage. Karol was quietest of all as she silently prayed that her beloved nephew Casey (at Karol's request, we changed his name) would walk through that door unharmed. He had suffered from no illness nor had an accident befallen him. He had not gotten into a fight or committed a crime.

Instead, an hour earlier, driving back from visiting his grandmother at her nursing home, a police officer had pulled him over on the side of the highway for failing to wear a seat belt. Now, long after the officer should have issued a warning or minor traffic ticket and sent Casey on his way, he had not arrived for Christmas dinner, and he wasn't answering his cell phone.

Karol's emotions hammered at her; she worried about what had happened and grew angrier and angrier at herself for failing to prevent it. She had witnessed the beginning of the incident.

From her own car, Karol saw Casey's car pulled over on the side of the road with a police car hovering behind it. So she too pulled over to check on him. As a senior member of the Obama Justice Department and former partner at Alston & Bird, a leading Atlanta law firm, Karol had deep experience with law enforcement. After what she had thought was a reassuring exchange with the police officer, she decided to drive away, leaving her nephew on his own to let the traffic stop run its course.

Now, though, her nephew had not returned. As a Black woman living in the South, Karol knew all too well that if a routine traffic stop went on for an hour, it might mean serious trouble. She didn't need the anxious looks and pointed questions from her family to make her wonder if she had made a terrible mistake by leaving Casey on his own.

Until that moment, Karol had made few mistakes in life. Certainly not big ones and not even many small ones. From childhood, she had looked after others and solved their problems. She had navigated through the upper echelons of corporate law and the Justice Department by astutely balancing the power she had earned with a keen understanding of how using her power could trigger a backlash. Over and over in her career she had made decisions that brought her clients and colleagues along with her rather than imposing her will on them. She was a "convener"—the person who gathered her family together, figured out how to defuse tense meetings at the office, and found a way to have an impact without leaving a large wake.

Growing up in Amityville on Long Island, Karol excelled from an early age and broke down barriers along the way. She and her brother were the first twins born in Lakeside Hospital. Why Lakeside when Brunswick Hospital was closer to their home? In the 1960s, Brunswick didn't treat Black people. It was like that a lot in their suburban life. Her parents moved to New York from North Carolina partly so they wouldn't face the redlining that prevented home ownership for many Black families, yet they only got their New York mortgage approved thanks to a friend who stuck their file in the middle of a pile of applications from White families.

Race, and its responsibilities, never felt far from their daily lives. There were only two Black doctors in Amityville, one of whom was brand-new to town. Karol's mother insisted that they use him just to help him succeed. The lesson stuck: Karol prioritized getting treated by Black doctors throughout her life.

While in high school, Karol taught with her mother at an adult-literacy program. Karol's parents never said explicitly that they needed to help other Black people; there was just an expectation—both positive and negative. Working hard in school and serving the community represented the positive roles to which they aspired. Conversely, Karol internalized "that if I messed up, I was messing things up for the race."

She and her siblings competed vigorously, with both their classmates and each other, for the best grades and longest list of compelling extracurriculars. She was a truly high performer.

Where some people have an understandably hard time in environments that highlight historical injustices or power imbalances, Karol adjusted through high achievement, acting "appropriately," and avoiding mistakes. By the time Karol applied to college, she had choices.

Her parents wanted her to attend a historically Black college. Karol wanted something larger and more diverse. They compromised on the University of North Carolina, where her parents felt that the Southern environment would give her a more "realistic" understanding of life as a Black woman in America.

That first year at college, she learned about more than race. Her roommate's boyfriend spent almost every night in their shared room. Half-jokingly, Karol reports that listening to the couple "traumatized" her. At a minimum, she didn't approve of their decisions. Going forward, she made sure to choose more like-minded suitemates, ones who kept visitors at bay by creating a less inviting climate for overnight visitors.

By junior year she had become a residence hall adviser. She majored in math and raced through her requirements even though the career choices it implied in finance and business held no interest for her. As a "child of the sixties and seventies" who grew up watching the news, she saw how "lawyers were the ones who changed the world, particularly at the Justice Department." As early as high school, Karol imagined herself in law school.

When she graduated from UNC, she once again had choices, and chose the University of Michigan Law School. The summer before her first year, she started what she thought would be her life's work by interning at the NAACP Legal Defense Fund. The work mattered and conformed with the activism she had witnessed from her parents. It also felt like the "right" place for a young Black lawyer.

Just as she hadn't met many Black doctors in Amityville, she had few legal role models. Growing up, the neighborhood lawyer handled everything from traffic tickets to divorces: not a life Karol imagined for herself. Then, during her summer internship, she met passionate civil rights lawyers whom she admired. So, Karol assumed that after law school she would return to Washington to pursue the advocacy work that had initially drawn her to the law.

Only after meeting Professor Sallyanne Payton, who was also Black, did Karol consider a corporate law career. Professor Payton told Karol that students such as her should consider corporate work as another way of advancing the very issues and priorities that had led Karol to spend a summer at the Legal Defense Fund.

In 1983, after a year in Chicago clerking for Judge John F. Grady, Karol joined Alston & Bird in Atlanta—a proper, white-shoe law firm that felt quite distant from the civil rights work that had initially drawn Karol to the law. Years later, when Karol made partner at Alston, a partner from their top competitor in Atlanta called to congratulate her. In the call, however, he subtly implied that Karol had gone to Alston only because she hadn't received an offer from his firm when she had graduated from law school.

Karol quickly corrected him. "I told him that I had received an offer. I chose Alston because I felt like they were more sincere. They weren't just checking a box. I just found it funny that he, in arrogance, thought that there's no way a Black woman would turn them down."

She didn't, however, tell him the other reason she hadn't gone to his firm. While she was a summer associate at that firm, the man who ran the program had driven Karol through a series of affluent, predominantly White Atlanta neighborhoods. The man told her, "If you come to work at our firm, this is where you can live."

Karol told him that she would actually prefer to live on the Black side of town. That he could not conceive of that preference heavily influenced her decision to join Alston.

It wasn't as if Alston had a large contingent of Black lawyers. There was one Black partner. And one Black female attorney, two years ahead of Karol. Perhaps four Black attorneys in total.

In 1990, Karol became Alston's first Black female partner.

Succeeding in a world where you're constantly the first and being held out as a role model for others to follow means enduring enormous pressure. Some people try to avoid those situations. Karol consistently sought them out.

"I have lived my life being the first of just about everything I've done professionally. So I don't have the luxury to make some mistakes. Of course, I've made them, but I am so aware that as the first Black woman . . . there are things that other people do that I just will never do. I follow rules, in particular, because it will have different ramifications if I don't."

Karol came to believe that her success depended on rule following: a schema that shaped much of her professional life.

Even while she built her legal practice, she found ways to stay engaged politically. When Barack Obama ran for president in 2008, Karol "worked her butt off" on his campaign. Despite developing close ties to President Obama's inner circle, she couldn't imagine going to work in Washington. She loved her work and personal life in Atlanta. She didn't mind the money either.

Yet, as more and more of her friends joined the administration, she rethought her decision. She didn't pursue it actively, but did hope that it would happen. Sure enough, the phone rang. The first call she received broached the idea of a federal judgeship: a plum assignment for any attorney committed to government service. Karol politely declined, as she didn't feel qualified.

Then one day while she visited friends in New York, Eric Holder, the attorney general designee, called to talk about jobs. Karol started the conversation with a direct question: "Who recommended me?" Well, Holder told her, just "Barack, Michelle, and Valerie [Jarrett]." While attending law school together, Karol and Jarrett had become close friends.

Holder's team and Karol went back and forth on her qualifications and interests. She made clear that she didn't want a job that required Senate confirmation, or one for which she wasn't clearly qualified.

Karol insisted that she would only take a job where her previous experience left her in a position to contribute meaningfully. She neither asked for nor received preferential treatment. In 2009, she became a deputy associate attorney general.

Even ignoring the backdrop of a global financial crisis, the Obama Justice Department had a strenuous first year. The Bush administration had implemented policies and pursued cases that the Democrats wanted to overturn while simultaneously beginning an ambitious affirmative agenda. Much of this work centered around Karol's areas of responsibility.

Because of her experience in public finance, the tax division reported to her. While she left the minutiae to her colleagues, they needed her involvement on high-level matters, especially international negotiations. Even something as arcane as international tax treaties, however, didn't allow Karol to escape the prejudice she had consistently experienced since childhood.

A delegation from the Swiss government came to discuss, no surprise, banking matters. During a tense moment in the negotiations, the lead Swiss representative stared at Karol, who was the only woman and only person of color in the room. Unaccustomed to probing questions, he said, "It's not like we're some African country."

Karol bit her tongue, reflected on her responsibility to negotiate a successful agreement rather than provoke an international incident, and, instead of addressing his comments directly, used them as motivation to negotiate forcefully on behalf of the United States.

Her behavior related partly to the schema that she developed over many years of living in a predominantly White world. It also reflected a completely new aspect in Karol's professional life: her two bosses—the attorney general and the president—were both Black.

"I never had had the experience of working for somebody of color. I was always the one Black person in the room with power." In any meeting, she felt that she didn't just represent the Justice Department, or the United States; she represented a milestone moment in American history for Black people, one that constantly activated her schema, reminding her that she couldn't afford to make mistakes.

Senior government jobs are hard. They're especially hard when you're trying to reform policies and cultures that date back hundreds of years. When you combine that with a deep sense of responsibility that comes from having the first Black attorney general and president, it creates a special kind of stress and a deep sensitivity to the intersection of race and responsibility.

In 1995, psychologists Claude Steele and Joshua Aronson performed the first of hundreds of experiments on stereotype threat, which occurs when a member of a marginalized group underperforms due to a fear of confirming negative stereotypes about the group.[1]

Steele and Aronson had African American and European American college students take a portion of the verbal section of the Graduate Record Examination (GRE). They split the students into two groups. Just before the verbal test, experimenters gave each group a survey about their demographic characteristics. The groups received identical surveys except that one group got asked their race at the end of the survey and the other group did not. Adjusting for their SAT scores, African American students who were asked their race performed worse than European American students or African American students who were not asked their race. Other research demonstrates that just being told the test is a diagnostic of ability can remind students of negative stereotypes, leading marginalized groups to perform more poorly.

It's not terribly surprising. Reminders of race or negative stereotypes about one's social groups can increase anxiety levels and even lead to physiological changes such as increased heart rate and blood pressure. That anxious arousal decreases attention to the task (e.g., getting distracted by worry or negativity). All of these totally under-standable reactions can reduce performance on the task.

Importantly, the inverse is also true. Sometimes reminding people of a negative stereotype explicitly causes them to want to disprove it, so they redouble their efforts and perform better than those not reminded of the negative stereotype. Psychologists call that stereotype reactance.[2] Research has shown how women—particularly Black women—feel forced to appear perfect with a "bulletproof" image.[3]

Karol is fully aware of how she has carried this burden throughout her career. She reached the highest levels of her profession with the satisfaction and the weight of often going first.

At each juncture, Karol took rational, careful steps to advance her career and the issues to which she felt committed. She knew that emotion, especially from Black women, was frequently and unfairly misinterpreted. Karol had developed a way of interacting with the world that allowed her to have success and that avoided the risk that others could use those stereotypes against her. She used facts and intense preparation to win substantive battles with people who too often relied on bluster and bias. All that control—her rule-following schema—took extraordinary effort and required real preparation and forethought.

It's a long, full Act I: a highly focused childhood in Amityville, exceptional academic achievement in college and law school, successful private legal practice, and then the Obama Justice Department. Karol spent her time before her mistake at the intersections of power and race, self-advancement and humility. She learned how to interact with the world and operate effectively within it: focus on the most important goals, avoid distracting "noise" even if offensive, and stay constantly vigilant about whom she represents.

With each new opportunity, Karol adjusted effectively to the new context. When she got approached about a judgeship, she suppressed her desires and focused on her qualifications. When a Swiss bureaucrat demonstrated bias, she kept the conversation focused on the law.

This smart, self-effacing, public-spirited woman had worked her way into a position of influence. By the time Karol returned to Atlanta for the holidays each year, she felt exhausted. Karol definitely needed time with her family to decompress, laugh, and shed the responsibilities she carried so diligently in her job. She needed a break from all that self-control.

Annually, the holiday started with a visit to Karol's mother in her nursing home, followed by a proper Christmas dinner at Karol's. Christmas 2013 was no different. After visiting with Karol's mother, the family cars—led by Casey in his new Ford—pulled onto the highway as they drove from Cobb County back to southwest Atlanta.

Shortly into the drive, Karol noticed Casey's car pulled to the side of the road with a police car parked behind it. She told her brother, Casey's uncle, to pull over so she could see what had happened.

She walked over to the officer and introduced herself as Casey's aunt. The officer responded, "Yeah, Auntie, he wasn't wearing his seat belt." The use of "Auntie" read two ways: affinity or condescension. The officer then took Casey's license back to the patrol car. Karol waited by the side of Casey's car. The officer waited in his car as he stared at his computer screen. And he kept waiting—showing no intention of getting out of his car while Karol stood there.

Given that the officer hadn't mentioned anything other than the seat belt, and that he appeared unwilling to resolve the matter while Karol lingered, she decided to leave. As she drove away with her brother, he told her that she'd made a mistake leaving their nephew alone. She disagreed and avoided the temptation to point out that he could have intervened if he felt so strongly.

They arrived home and repeatedly tried Casey's phone with no success. As the minutes ticked away and Casey hadn't rejoined them,

Karol, who enjoyed a loving but competitive relationship with her brother, painfully came to agree with him: she had made a bad mistake leaving Casey alone with the police.

Finally, Casey arrived back home. He was "cussing and fussing." Like many people when they're deeply worried, Karol reacted with fear.

"Please tell me," she snapped, "that you didn't speak to the officer like that."

To his credit, Casey calmed down and explained that the officer had called for backup that included police dogs and several other squad cars. For an hour, and for no discernible reason, they had treated him as a dangerous criminal. Karol's earlier presence and Casey's respectful reaction to the initial traffic stop had done nothing to deter an intensely aggressive reaction from the police.

Casey's description left Karol deeply shaken. Both Casey's father and Karol were single at the time, so Karol played "the mom role." The incident felt particularly hard partly because of how she perceived their relationship. She also worried about how it would affect Casey's relationship with law enforcement and his sense of self.

"I thought, 'He would never trust an officer again.'"

Why had Karol misread the situation and made the mistake of leaving him alone?

As a first part of the answer, try to picture the scene: a young Black man gets stopped in Cobb County, Georgia—an affluent, two-thirds Caucasian area outside Atlanta. Imagine that officer calling for backup that included police dogs. Now try to picture the officer.

If you imagine a White officer, that may reflect your learned experience or knowledge of probabilities, or it may signify some unconscious bias.

Or you may have considered why Karol felt comfortable leaving the scene. Perhaps the officer was Black and Karol experienced affinity bias: the phenomenon of trusting and liking people who are like ourselves.

The officer, like Karol and Casey, was Black.

"I thought, 'Okay, it's a Black officer who knows Casey's got a family member who cares about him. . . . It's going to be okay. . . . He's not profiling my nephew.'" Perhaps the officer's use of the word "auntie" also reinforced that perceived affinity and could have activated Karol's schema that Black people look after other Black people. Or maybe she had misinterpreted the tone of the word and he had used it to patronize her.

Karol immediately acknowledges that race played a role in her decision. "Had that been a White officer, I wouldn't have left. In the South, we—and by that I mean Black people—sort of have this code of honor with each other and code of trust."

Conversely, given her career in law enforcement and general tendency to show grace, Karol later recognized the limitations of that affinity. "The officer's loyalty was to the badge first and not to his race. So that doesn't make him a bad person. I expected a level of empathy from him that I didn't get."

Whether conscious or unconscious, her expectation led to her misinterpreting the situation. She had a lifelong cognitive reaction to Black people in positions of power. Karol assumed something—based on years of lived experience—that proved painfully untrue.

If you're raised to trust the Black doctor, if you're mentored by Black women who care deeply about your professional success, if you're working for the first Black president, it's hardly surprising that you would expect to find affinity with a Black police officer who's handling something as minor as a traffic violation.

She had a schema about the world that she had learned from her childhood: a schema that had served her well until it didn't.

Just that year, she had started a new job at the Justice Department where she was responsible for everything that related to state and local criminal justice issues. She oversaw the Bureau of Justice Assistance, which funds state and local government programs in areas such as victims' rights, juvenile justice, and statistical collection and analysis. To understate her influence, her position gave her real relevance to the situation and the local police department.

Karol could easily have tried to use her influence to get the officer to waive the ticket altogether or at least issue it quickly so Casey could head off to Christmas dinner. She chose not to even mention her status. In those few moments by the side of the road, she quickly calculated the risk of using her influence if it ever became public.

"I didn't want to create any distractions for President Obama. So that was more of a factor in my mind than anything else. I didn't want anybody saying, 'Oh, you think because you work in that administration, you can do what you want to do.'"

She had an ambivalent attitude toward influence. She didn't want to parlay her personal relationships for professional advantage, or vice versa. She'd also learned, however, that in certain situations a strategic approach could help address systemic power imbalances. She had learned that from her mother. While her mother could become deeply emotional at home, she knew how to control her emotions and channel them when needed.

"My mother modeled how to deal with people in power and authority. At our school, there were teachers that were notoriously not good, and at the beginning of the school year, she would go up there to the main office at the school and say that her children will not have these teachers. And we didn't have those teachers. She was an active parent about making sure we got what we needed."

As her career advanced, Karol became comfortable with using her own power. "But for the fact that I was in the Obama administration, I would have used my strictly lawyer power and relationship power without any hesitation. Because one of the things I do feel very strongly about is that, as Black people, we are finally in a position where we've got the ability to make things happen and protect our families and use relationships to give opportunities. But that one was complicated because I was in the Obama administration.

"I have been told by other communities of color they have a similar thing. We all know we represent the race when we have these jobs. We can't afford to mess up because then we make it difficult for anybody coming behind us." For Karol, it meant avoiding the risk that anyone would ever suggest that she had used her position to benefit a relative.

So much went into shaping Karol's reaction. Years of conditioning made her inclined to trust the Black officer. She'd also developed a successful schema for how to handle situations that involved power, race, and the law. More often than not, it was best to swallow her fears, to show deference to people in positions of power, and to suppress whatever annoyance she might feel in order to achieve a bigger goal.

She also felt an intense sense of responsibility to her bosses in the Obama administration and the broader Black community. She hated the thought of embarrassing them, which meant that despite having achieved status and power herself, she felt deeply constrained in how she could use it. Ironically, the decision to help others through public service made it more difficult for her to help someone she loved in the very situation that she hoped to reform.

Immediately after her mistake, Karol felt the consequences: Casey's anger, her guilt, her family's fear. It made her miserable at the time and for years to come.

Act III began with what at first seemed like a new mistake: her inability to forgive herself. Karol loved Casey as her own child—ever since he had come into her life when she was thirty-five. Years later, the 2016 presidential campaign reinforced the incident.

"A lot of young Black men, including Casey, could not vote for Hillary Clinton because of the ads that they ran on the Black radio stations with her calling young Black men 'superpredators.'"

In the years since the incident, after listening to others, Karol has partially adjusted the way she thinks about what happened.

"Mayor Garcetti [the former mayor of Los Angeles] told me that his grandfather was an immigrant and, when he was young, often got in trouble. One day his grandfather got stopped by Tom Bradley, who was then a police officer [and later became mayor]. Bradley, who was just a young patrol officer at that point, said to Garcetti's grandfather, 'You've got so much more potential than this. You're running with the wrong crowd. You need to get your life in order.'

"I don't know if that traffic stop actually turned around the grandfather's life. But it feels like it might have had a generational impact. That immigrant's son went on to become the first Latinx DA in California, and then his son becomes the mayor. That's how it's supposed to work. Not like what happened to Casey."

As part of her work at the Justice Department and then as president of John Jay College, the country's leading higher education institution focused on criminal justice, she began to tell the Casey story as a way to help people understand the need for reform.

"My approach is that I'm just going to tell the story and keep telling the story so that people understand how one encounter can have community impact, even generational impact, on what people think about law enforcement."

Karol would never suggest that she was "glad" that Casey got stopped. Yet while listening to her story, it's impossible not to wonder how the experience has helped others, given the passion she has brought to her work. In a sense, even though she felt deeply committed to criminal justice reform before the incident, her evolution reflects a form of posttraumatic growth: the way trauma can lead some people to gain deeper understanding, increased resilience, and new perspectives.[4]

She knows that if you really want people to hear you, they need to connect emotionally. By sharing her story, she allows her mistake to serve a higher purpose. That helps not only her audience, but also her own healing.

"Whenever I do talk about it, I'm not afraid or ashamed to show emotion. I tell people all the time, 'I'm a sixty-four-year-old woman, and I'm okay crying in front of people.'"

Karol has chosen not to talk with Casey about the incident. That may relate, at least partially, to her difficulty in forgiving herself.

"I haven't forgiven myself because what happened never leaves me. Maybe on an intellectual level I probably have forgiven myself, but on a really deep level, no. It still hurts that I let that happen to him.

"I feel like I'm doing penance every day by trying to fix it. I'll forgive myself when I can make sure this doesn't happen to anybody else's little boy."

For Karol, forgiveness comes through the work. Rather than channeling her emotional reaction into anger, she has tried to channel it into reform. She wears the responsibility heavily.

"I think mistakes that really hurt other people or cause other people harm, those are different."

As hard as she works, the load doesn't get lighter. It's hard not to wonder how much of her mistake really relates to her, and how much to the country in which we live. Throughout her life, she has sailed into the constant headwinds of systemic racism and misogyny. And that defines her.

When asked, Karol described herself as "Black is always first. Always first."

Before woman?

"Oh yeah. When we used to have things at the firm, when they talked about women, I'd have to tell people, 'You know the gender piece isn't a factor for me. Race is predominant.'"

And what comes next after identifying herself as Black? "Probably lawyer, even before woman." Of course, identity is highly contextual. How she perceives herself with her family differs from her role in meetings with foreign tax experts, which in turn differs from working at a law firm.

Karol reflected some more and adjusted her view. "Black. Woman. Probably lawyer, not in terms of what I do, but in terms of how I process and move through the world. Then friend. Family."

That Christmas Day, by the side of a road in Cobb County, Georgia, all those roles ran right into one another. Was she an aunt? A lawyer? A powerful woman? A representative of all the progress Black people have made? A survivor of all the progress the country has failed to make? Someone who is expected to only use her influence in exactly the right way at the right moment?

Despite all of the deep societal complexity, notwithstanding the absence of a "good" option, Karol clearly feels that she made a mistake. One that's stayed with her. "It can just be overwhelming to have to deal with this every time you turn around. There's somebody else abusing their authority or their power. How are we making sure these things never happen again?

"Sometimes I just need a break from all this stuff because I feel it too deeply. Sometimes it feels like there's no solution to it, but then I pick myself back up and say, 'Okay. I got it, I'm not giving up.'"

10

Three's Company

I t's no wonder that academics study *Cosmopolitan* magazine when they write about American feminism. The magazine started in 1886 as a "family" magazine with what the publisher describes as "a department devoted exclusively to the interests of women, with articles on fashion, on household decorations, on cooking, on household management and the care and management of children."[1]

A decade later, it hired alumni from *Harper's Weekly* to pursue a more literary focus that included articles and stories by authors such as Willa Cather, Rudyard Kipling, Jack London, and Edith Wharton. The inclusion of women authors gave the first hint of the wholesale change that would follow.

Under William Randolph Hearst's ownership, which began at the turn of the century, *Cosmo* solidified its position in the literary world. Then, in the 1950s, the literary genre began to decline under increasing pressure from television and other lighter forms of entertainment.

By the 1960s, circulation had plummeted; *Cosmo* needed a reboot. Enter Helen Gurley Brown, author of *Sex and the Single Girl*, ardent feminist, and unabashed advocate for female sexuality and empower-ment. From 1965 to 1997, readers knew what to expect: frank advice about sex and dating, and insights into careers and health (some of which—especially around AIDS—was, alas, dead wrong).

The promotion of Joanna Coles, the editor of *Marie Claire*, to run *Cosmo* in 2012 signaled a shift of direction. Joanna had a distin-guished journalistic pedigree. Having published her first article in *The Yorkshire Post* at the age of ten, she went on to work for *The Specta-tor*, *The Daily Telegraph*, and *The Guardian* before taking over *Marie Claire*. There, among other accomplishments, she expanded it with the launch of *Marie Claire @Work*, which focused on fashion and style in the workplace. The last title reflected what would become one of her abiding interests—one that would set a new path for *Cosmo*.

Under her leadership, while the covers maintained their embrace of female sexuality, the articles reflected Joanna's focus on the intersec-tion of women's private and professional lives. Within eighteen months of her assuming leadership, *Cosmo* won its first prestigious National Magazine Award for public service journalism. Joanna had not only published a twelve-page graphic feature on birth control, but also used traditional *Cosmo* topics as a gateway to important adjacent issues such as how to save for a down payment. Both showed Joanna's focus on independence and self-determination.

She came to those topics with more than an abstract interest. You don't move from West Yorkshire, in England's dying industrial heart-land, to Fleet Street, the most raucous, male-dominated bastion in journalism—or from Fleet Street to Madison Avenue, the most rarefied publishing environment—without a capacity for self-determination. At least from the outside, Joanna seemed to have made all the right moves. Not only did she achieve ever-greater professional success, she fell in love, got married, moved from London to New York, and had two healthy boys with whom she remains close.

While things didn't always go perfectly—at *Marie Claire*, for example, she got embroiled in a controversy over fat-shaming—she's that rare publishing executive whose public persona is notable more for the absence of crises than their presence. To the extent that there were professional mistakes—the inevitable missed deadlines, misconstrued facts, flubbed launches—they left her emotions and reputation remarkably unscathed. She even avoided the perils that befall many people who live such full lives: she didn't ignore health issues, lose friendships, or become annoyingly snarky.

Yes, she got divorced, but there too she avoided the toxicity that befalls many uncoupled people. She lives as she appears: straightforward and straight ahead.

When we asked about the biggest mistake in her life, we had no idea what she would choose, as nothing seemed obvious from the outside.

She wanted to talk about children. Not the difficulty of raising them. Nor the mistakes she made as a parent or the way her work conflicted with parenting. No, the mother of two healthy young men wanted to talk about numbers. "I wish that I had had at least one, if not two, more children."

Joanna had traveled a long way to get to where she felt so comfortable writing and talking about sex. West Yorkshire in the 1960s was a good century removed from the mores and vitality of *Cosmo*'s headquarters. Rationing, a relic of World War II, ended less than ten years before Joanna's birth, and the economy never regained the glory of the industrial revolution. Joanna has no nostalgia about the environment. "Everybody I knew who grew up in the north of England was trying to leave because it was a fairly depressing place. There were miner strikes, there were blackouts, there were brownouts. Britain was kind of depressed."

It was there that a young Joanna began a journalism career that almost veered into public service. "I wrote an essay about climate change when I was seventeen that won an *Observer* newspaper prize. And as a result, the local Green Party came to me to see if I would be interested in standing as a Green councilor. . . . My parents said, 'Absolutely not. You're not going to stand as a councilor and not go to college. You have to go to college.'"

It wasn't as if her parents' college dreams rested on her shoulders. Her mother had a serious, full-time job while simultaneously managing the household, a true second shift before the term existed. It required careful organization, right down to what they ate every night. "Every Monday . . . we always had stew. Every Tuesday, chops. Every Wednesday, salad. Thursday, risotto. Friday, fish and chips."

Joanna remembers the claustrophobia that permeates the lives of so many smart, ambitious adolescents in less than fully invigorating environments. "Life just felt very dull. You got up, you went to school, you did your schoolwork, and then you're kind of constantly looking for other things that would be more interesting." Life did not include long conversations about emotions.

Her mother's cooking and routines, which must have taken astonishing energy, seem quite different in hindsight. "Now I look back on it, and I think how extraordinary that my mom made breakfast every morning. She cooked us dinner every single night. And, of course, I was completely unappreciative of that. At the time, it felt sort of oppressive.

"I remember her just being exhausted all the time and thinking, 'Well, I will earn more money, so that I will have more help.'"

After college, she got her first job at *The Spectator* and then migrated to the more mainstream press. "My interview at *The Daily Telegraph* with Max Hastings, the editor, lasted exactly a minute and a half. He looked at me and said, 'I haven't read your résumé. But you're under thirty, and you're a woman, and we need both of those. So you're in.' I just said, 'Fantastic! So excited!' My résumé was very short. I had two years at *The Spectator*. I felt very wanted because I was a reasonably smart young woman, and the world was opening up to people like us. We had—I had so much opportunity."

While her gender helped open that door, it became more complicated as she rose in seniority.

The companies for which she worked, and the men who ran them, wanted to hire women. They knew they "needed" them for political reasons. Some even got it more fundamentally: the importance of a diversity of views, the value of talent that had gone underutilized, the need to have teams that reflected the composition of their audiences. Yet, they still sent clear messages about their expectations that work had to come before family.

"I always wanted to move to America, and I didn't want to have a child before I got here because it would make it harder to send me. If you're on a foreign desk, it's much harder to send women with kids than send men with kids. I just think there's an inherent bias against it, or perhaps that's what I perceive. Perhaps that's untrue.

"But when I look back at the female foreign correspondents at *The Guardian*, I don't think there were any in a post with children when I was sent to New York . . . as the bureau chief for *The Guardian*. I got pregnant within the first year, so I was thirty-six."

When her oldest son was a toddler, two Dartmouth professors were murdered in their homes. The story made national headlines in the United States and, due to the horrific violence in a pastoral setting, wormed its way into the British consciousness as well. Her editors wanted her in New Hampshire to cover it, which would have meant missing her son's second birthday. "So I called the paper and said, 'I'll go up to New Hampshire, but I'm not going to go up today. I'll go up tomorrow.' And they said, 'No, you have to go today. It's a huge story. Blah blah blah.' So I missed his birthday party."

She ended up staying in New Hampshire longer than expected, and then the paper didn't run the piece for three days. It brought about two realizations. She no longer wanted to be "rushing off to do stories that didn't seem as significant as spending time with my children."

And the experience writing about the murders after missing the birthday party made her think differently about the fragility of life.

"The randomness of those crimes and the nudge to treat every day as a gift. That doesn't sound too Hallmark? But, you know, when you cover stories as a journalist, you get real insight into the underbelly of life." Some people witness a traumatic event without experiencing a meaningful reorientation of their outlook or priorities. For others, the impact presents itself in the future, and only with hindsight does the event feel meaningful. For Joanna, it hit right away. She decided to switch from her job as a reporter to magazine editor, where she would have more control over her daily schedule.

While her desire to have children had not influenced her career path previously, for the first time, in her late thirties, she reordered her priorities. She kept advancing professionally—editorship at *Marie Claire*, which led to *Cosmo*, which led to her becoming the chief content officer of Hearst—but she also began to reassess her attitudes toward motherhood. "The moment I had [my first son], I thought, 'Oh, goodness! Why on earth didn't I do this earlier? This is so much more profound than I had expected.'"

So, why hadn't she done it earlier? Part of the decision related to the aforementioned impediments for women who, for example, wanted overseas assignments.

Part of it relates to the constraints she internalized. "I grew up in a generation of women that were indoctrinated about really focusing on their career at the expense of everything else."

Those women, real and fictional, often didn't have children. "Mary Tyler Moore looked like the most sophisticated, exciting lifestyle you could possibly hope to aspire to as a young woman. My goal was eventually to get to America and sort of live out a Mary Tyler Moore fantasy."

Joanna's fantasy of a single woman focused almost exclusively on her work and social life partly reflected a schema about how to cope with the myriad demands that working women faced. Her mother solved for the complexity of her life through discipline and planning. And her children understood their role. "We didn't really argue. I wasn't a difficult teenager. . . . Our home was sort of ordered and quiet. I had always wanted more siblings. I envied bigger families and the sort of noise and the chaos . . . a mild riot of kids around."

She may have longed for "chaos" or a "mild riot," but she actually led her life with extraordinary discipline and prioritization. Some of which she clearly regrets. Without expressing blame, she thinks expansively about the causes.

"In the background I was reading books by female authors and female journalists. . . . Someone like Martha Gellhorn felt like an interesting role model. People weren't really discussing children. The pill had meant that people had freedom from worrying about being pregnant. And you suddenly had this sense of the world opening up to women in a way that it hadn't done before and that it was your duty to take advantage of it."

"I think part of the women's movement really looked down on women who had children. And I'm not sure that they were entirely honest about it."

When you hear the same message from the male patriarchy at work and some of your feminist role models, it has an effect. Well before she began to write about birth control, she recognized how the message about prioritizing work influenced not just personal behavior, but also the obligations she felt as a feminist.

In 2012, Anne-Marie Slaughter, the first female director of policy planning at the State Department, wrote what would become a seminal article in *The Atlantic*. At the time she wrote it, she had a son almost exactly the same age as Joanna's. Slaughter's title captured perfectly the essence of her article and how so many women felt: "Why Women Still Can't Have It All."[2]

The article is filled with quotes that relate to Joanna's "mistake." Slaughter wrote, "Women of my generation have clung to the feminist credo we were raised with, even as our ranks have been steadily thinned by unresolvable tensions between family and career, because we are determined not to drop the flag for the next generation."

Slaughter also understood clearly the impact of educational and economic status. "I am writing for my demographic—highly educated, well-off women who are privileged enough to have choices in the first place."

Joanna echoes that sentiment and quickly acknowledges that American society still hasn't provided adequate childcare options. "I know this is a very White-privileged conversation, and that there are women out there holding down three jobs with five kids. So I want to be respectful of that. I just feel a little sad that the culture didn't allow us to have that maneuverability that men had."

She puts part of her evolution down to age. "The idea that you would not have children because you have some kind of loyalty to a corporation is one of those things that you can sell to people in their twenties and thirties. But the longer you spend in a working life, the more you realize that's absurd and that corporations have very little loyalty to people."

She mentors countless women informally, has helped even more of them build their careers, and can't help getting frustrated around some women when they talk about having children. "The first thing that comes out of their mouth is 'Oh, it's too hard.' And the second is that they want their career. And when I ask them what the career is, the career is never anything that you think, 'Why on earth would this be the reason that you can't have children?'"

As Joanna grew older, the issue grew in complexity. She felt the very real conflict with her work but recognized something deeper: how to balance self and other.

"We've created this paradigm—I mean, in the Western world—where we encouraged people to think a lot about themselves and go inside themselves. And what I think you realize as you get older is that that's not actually a path to happiness.

"I felt that I was part of a generation of women who were encouraged to think a lot about ourselves. And part of the disadvantage of having a child would be that we would think less about ourselves."

For many driven people of Joanna's generation, "thinking" about themselves generally meant thinking about how to accomplish their objectives. They saw themselves in relation to their work and colleagues; accomplishments served as a crucial barometer of how successfully they had channeled their emotions and energy. In the 1980s, books such as *The 7 Habits of Highly Effective People*, *The One Minute Manager*, and *In Search of Excellence* generated intense followings.

The civic and business leaders Joanna covered, and the bosses who guided her professional development, had relatively narrow definitions of success.

She worries that as a society we send the wrong message around having children. "You think you're not going to be able to do this because there won't be enough energy. But it's as if you go through a sort of trapdoor, and there's more space than you realized. It's like finding an extra room that you didn't think was there. And you find, you know, different chambers in your heart that create more connection to the world actually."

After Joanna gave birth to her son, she found herself caring much more about that connection to the world: she lifted her head up and not only liked what she saw, but also realized what she had lost as part of her move to the US.

As much as she has succeeded in her new setting, she cannot shake a certain sense of dislocation and longing for elements of England.

Despite having lived in the United States for thirty years, Joanna still defines herself partly by her immigrant status. "There is a sort of sense of displacement that I underestimated . . . I wish I had moved to America earlier in my life too.

"This may be a sort of immigrant fantasy. I miss my family in the UK. And so, perhaps if we'd had more children, it would make me feel like we had a stronger foothold in America. . . . It would resemble or symbolize a stronger sense of belonging in the US. I know lots of immigrant families feel like that.

"So part of this may actually be my disconnection or change of citizenship halfway through my life actually, which I'd never thought of before, but that could well be part of it." In important ways, children, and their worlds, compensate for what she left behind. "You become part of a school community, which felt important to me. You become aware of a whole host of difficulties that other families go through. It's the great humbling having children. It's a great leveler. And I think that's a very reassuring stage to go through in life."

Her work life, while meaningful, clearly provides less emotional engagement. "It's a more transactional community when you're in a corporate environment."

She returns again and again to the idea of how to create community: sometimes in relation to our society ("I think we've completely undermined in our culture the significance of family and the importance of family") and often much more personally ("I'm not involved in a church or a temple, so I don't have those communities. But I feel like I've built my own communities").

If you're an immigrant, and you feel that neither work nor religion provides a deeply fulfilling sense of belonging, and if, as Joanna said, "there's a kind of ebb and flow of friendships depending on where you all are in your life," then family becomes even more important.

In 1980, Toni Antonucci and Robert Kahn, from the University of Michigan, wrote about social convoy theory, the idea that our happiness depends partly on whether we have a group of people who accompany us over time. They articulated circles of relationship from the closest (e.g., family and lifelong friends) to the weakest (e.g., a barista to whom we say hello to each morning). We move through life with our convoy; some people enter our circle, others drop out. Once lifelong friends drop out, however, it's almost impossible to replace them. We can't go back to childhood and start over.

By moving to the United States, Joanna experienced an acute break with the inner circle of her convoy. She didn't have family or lifelong friends in the United States, but she could add children—the ultimate members of her inner circle. She could rebuild from the inside out: "The family becomes its own community in a different way, and you rely on it more."

As she's gained the wisdom that comes with experience, she has realized the fulfillment that comes from creating and nurturing things and people beyond ourselves. Her changed perspective relates to what prominent psychologist and Harvard professor Erik Erikson described as the stage of generativity versus stagnation in his landmark book *Childhood and Society* (the stage right before integrity versus despair that we referenced earlier). He argued that in the middle-adulthood years, people typically find happiness and satisfaction in generativity, creating and nurturing things and people that will outlive us.

With unusual insight, Joanna has the ability to step outside herself to analyze these crosscurrents. When we pressed her on how she *felt* about her decision not to have more children, as opposed to the *reasons* why she did not, she drew upon the schema that had helped her survive Fleet Street when she first started her career.

"You know that I'm British, right? British people don't have feelings. I'm being very effective at resisting [the question] 'How do I feel about it?' I feel like I wish I had . . . I wish I'd had more, you know? I don't feel sad about it as much as just slightly regretful actually."

Joanna's quintessentially British disconnect from her emotions is hardly uncommon, and, in fairness, the importance of using our emotional skills has only received attention relatively recently because of Peter Salovey and John Mayer's four-branch model of emotional intelligence.[3] Their work became the basis for so many popular articles, books, and corporate executive trainings that we forget that they published their findings in 1990.

Beneath all her intellect lay deep reserves of perspective—"I'm very happy to say that I'm fantasizing about the lost objects very clearly"—and practicality. So much so that she believes that Kate Middleton's mother did the right thing by arranging for her daughter to transfer to St. Andrews to secure her relationship with Prince William. We could hear genuine wistfulness coupled with humor when she said, "I was so jealous of Martin Amis when he discovered a kind of fully forged child that he didn't know he had. I just thought, 'What a great gift!'" (Amis famously learned that a brief affair had produced a daughter about whom he didn't know until she was a teenager.)

As much as she joked during our conversation, nothing could hide her deep maternal love. She laughs warmly as she describes how her sons had overheard our conversation: "I think one of them said, 'I can't believe you're landing this on me today,' and then wandered off. I told him that I was just showing that I like you both, and I wanted more. And he said, 'Well, just hope for lots of grandchildren.'"

11

To *Elle* and Back

Note: The interviews with Irv Gotti occurred more than a year before his tragic death from diabetes in 2025. Irv's family has approved the use of those interviews and the clarifications of his quotes and confirmed his recollection of the events that he described.

One morning in 2001, Irv Gotti, the legendary artist and producer, got a call from Tommy Mottola, the longtime CEO of Sony Music. "I'm like, 'Tommy, what's up? It's so fucking early.' He's like, 'I need you to make a record . . . make a record with J.Lo. And put Ja [Rule] on it and make it a duet.'"

The song, "I'm Real," debuted at number 66 on the Hot 100 that July. By September 1, it was the number one song in America. So began an amazing collaboration with Jennifer Lopez that less than two years later Irv burned to the ground. He made a mistake for which he had still not forgiven himself when we interviewed him.

Before he became Irv Gotti, or DJ Irv, he was Irving Domingo Lorenzo Jr.—one of eight children growing up in Queens. As in many large families, Irv's older siblings had very different experiences from the younger ones. His five sisters, who had traditional middle-income childhoods, "weren't in the hood. When they went to party, they would party in the city—in Manhattan."

Irv's own early years felt quite different. "I grew up in the hood. It was all Black. So there wasn't a lot of White people where I grew up. Everyone was selling crack, and everyone was violent."

From an early age, and then throughout his career, Irv had to navigate two separate and still-intertwined worlds: Queens, where Irv lived and drew inspiration for his music, and Manhattan, where the executives who controlled the industry lived and partied.

As he grew older, Irv migrated to Manhattan and achieved remarkable success. First, through collaborations with the biggest hip-hop artists such as Jay-Z, who gave him the nickname Gotti. Why Gotti? Jay-Z wanted to "toughen him up," to highlight his intensity and leadership in the style of the famed mob boss. Following this collaboration, and others like it, Irv got his own labels—Murder Inc. and The Inc.

That success led to the early-morning call from Mottola and the relationship with J.Lo. The friendship between J.Lo and Irv originated, like many great unions, out of anger, but not between them.

In 2001, Mariah Carey recorded a song with Ja Rule and Irv for the movie *Glitter*. Tommy Mottola heard about the collaboration before it got released. Mottola, who had gotten divorced from Carey a few years earlier, made that early-morning call because, according to Irv, Mottola "wanted to beat Mariah to the punch of having a duet produced by Murder Inc. with Ja Rule on it."

Why did Mottola want Irv to work with J.Lo? Irv believes that Mottola knew Irv had a single-minded approach to his music. "When I make music, my first thought is to make it hot. Make that shit hot. Make it so people got to listen to it, and they want it over and over and over again."

On the same day as his call, Mottola and his new wife, Thalía, came to Irv's studio. The elevator didn't work, so they had to climb six flights of stairs. Mottola didn't arrive in a good mood and said, "This fucking record better be fucking good."

"I play 'I'm Real' for him. Him and his wife go crazy. They're like, 'Oh, my God!' It was a one-listen! So he puts me on a private jet. I fly to LA. We record the record with J.Lo. We shoot the video. Next thing you know, the record comes out. It's all over the radio. I'm talking about maybe a couple of days after we recorded it, it's all over the radio."

After "I'm Real" goes to number one, they went from hit to hit. "Ain't It Funny" followed, and it too made it to number one. "Those records was colossal, not just in the States. On the planet Earth! I don't give a fuck if you went to Germany, Australia, Africa; that shit was in heavy rotation."

Irv worried about how J.Lo would work in his environment. She nailed it from the moment she walked into Irv's studio. "She was straight Jenny from the block. She was looking like a bad bitch from the Bronx. She had every one of my guys fall in love with her. She could have been on some 'I'm a big star' bougie shit, but she was the total opposite.

"She worked the whole room. When she left, every guy was like, 'Yo, she's dope. I think she liked me.' I'm like, 'Yo, dog. She worked us, yo.'"

The combination of number one records, personal connection, and genuine respect led to an unusually strong collaboration. "Benny Medina [J.Lo's manager] was telling Sony, 'Irv Gotti is going to be our Quincy Jones. . . . We're not doing no music unless Irv is involved.'"

Unless you grew up around the music industry, it's hard to appreciate how much Irv had achieved. He had worked with the most influential artists in his genre, he had transitioned into working with crossover stars, and he had built relationships of deep trust and respect with the managers and executives who wield enormous power.

He had traveled so far and would have done almost anything to preserve his position. Certainly, a small favor for someone as important as J.Lo. So when *Elle* magazine wanted to put her on the cover and she asked Irv to give a quote for the story, he happily agreed.

The reporter didn't catch Irv at his best. "The *Elle* magazine guy calls me to say, 'I'm such and such for *Elle* magazine. J.Lo told me to call you.' I immediately respond with 'Yeah, what the fuck you want?'"

That's not the kind of response that *Elle* reporters expect, especially ones who write flattering celebrity profiles. The reporter cut immediately to his key question: J.Lo had told him that 'I'm Real' and 'Ain't It Funny' were *not* about Puff Daddy, her ex-boyfriend. Did Irv agree?

"What?!" Irv responded. "That bitch is lying."

Shortly thereafter, Irv's quote appeared in print right after J.Lo's. Unsurprisingly, that ended the friendship and the collaboration, "It's the worst mistake I've ever made in my life." With one very ill-advised comment, he had gone from comparisons to Quincy Jones to persona non grata.

He didn't just mourn the professional loss; he felt the pain acutely because of the relationship too. "She was my friend. The biggest star in the world was one of my good friends."

It seems implausible that in the midst of one of the most successful collaborations in music history, Irv would blow up the relationship over something as trivial as the origin story of a hit song.

It didn't help that by his own acknowledgment he took too many drugs during that moment in his life, but he didn't blame being high. Other factors had a much deeper influence on his frame of mind.

"I was like on top of the world. It was a feeling of invincibility. It was a feeling of I could do whatever the fuck I want. That's to portray who I was at that moment. I'm from the hood. I got the Midas touch. All of my records are working and going number one. I could do no wrong."

Irv wasn't wrong. He had huge commercial success across several genres creating enormous value for the artists and their labels. Not only did he have talent; he also had power and independence. "I don't need nobody. Y'all need me. I don't need y'all."

Could those feelings of power and invincibility have made him speak more freely to the reporter? Perhaps, although Irv expressed such affection for J.Lo that it seems unlikely that his ego led him to trash her.

So why did he do it? Right before his conversation with the *Elle* reporter, Irv had spoken about an unrelated matter with a highly influential record executive—the kind of person who had real influence on Irv's work and livelihood. Irv was in a good mood when the executive called him. "It wasn't like I was in some militant mood watching fucking Malcolm X. I was in the studio, creating, mastering an album, having a good time."

The conversation ended minutes before the *Elle* reporter called and left "steam coming out of my ears. I'm heated." It began with a tense but businesslike discussion about a record that featured J.Lo and Ja Rule and that originally included Caddillac Tah, another rapper, on both the record and in the accompanying video. The label had removed Caddillac from the record while leaving him in the video. Irv didn't understand or appreciate the decision to leave him off the record.

Irv cared deeply about Caddillac's treatment. "I was pissed. 'Why are you hurting me? Just leave him on the record. They'll play the record.' And the executive says, 'I just want it to be J.Lo and Ja.'

"And I'm like, 'Well, why'd you let me shoot the video with Caddy in it? You're sending mixed signals to radio and making my artist look wack by not servicing it with him on the record.'"

Suddenly, from a heated, but not unusual, conversation in the music industry, everything fell apart when the executive blamed one of his colleagues.

Irv had a clear recollection of what happened next. The executive's may differ. Irv remembers him saying, "I told that fat N-word, [name deleted], to not do this."

Irv was shocked. "What the fuck you say? Did you just call [him] a [N-word]? When this N-word see you, I'm gonna fuck you up."

The experience brought back a painful memory from Irv's adolescence. One of Irv's sisters had dated a tough Italian American who would invite Gotti to play in pickup basketball games at the Downtown Athletic Club in Manhattan. Irv, at only fifteen years old, "used to torch these guys. . . . We keep winning, keep killing them, and I'm killing them in a hood way, very flashy."

The college boys "got mad and angry." Irv could tell it wasn't just about his style of play. They asked his sister's boyfriend about Irv. "You could tell they wanted to say, 'Who brought these N-words?'"

Instead, they asked, "Who brought these Black kids? They're disrupting our basketball game."

Years later, after conquering Manhattan and the music industry, the story feels fresh as he describes how he responded to the insults. "I took the ball, and I weaved my way around the pick. . . . I was basically like, 'I'm just gonna take this motherfucker in front of me,' which I did and hit the game winner. And, oh, they was mad."

It's basketball as combat: Gotti as a fifteen-year-old taking on the world—or, more important, the power structures that dominated it. He formed a schema that lasted for decades; he would play the game his way and never let prejudice go unchallenged.

Not since the basketball game at the Downtown Athletic Club had Irv experienced such an overtly racist comment.

"I'd never experienced that before where someone will use the term 'N-word' in front of me."

Irv felt deeply disrespected. "But where he fucked up is who the fuck you think you're talking to? I'm not one of your workers. I'm a Black man. I'm a Black man that delivered two colossal number one records to you. Who the fuck you think you are that gives you the right to use the N-word around me?"

Irv did not feel remorseful about what he said to the executive. "I'm not a volatile person. But when it comes to somebody like this powerful guy saying the N-word, you're gonna see. You're gonna see the worst of Irv Gotti!"

The executive's comment would have offended anyone, but Irv had particularly strong views about race and power.

He reflected deeply on the country's racist history. "People ask me would I be able to operate in those times of racism? And I always answer, 'I would die.' Because I couldn't take the racism that would have been bestowed upon me. I couldn't take them doing something to my mother or hanging my father and I'm living life. No, you're gonna have to kill me too."

He knew what happened to young Black men who spoke the truth. "So if I came up during that time, I would have probably died as a young boy. I would have got hung and got killed as a young boy because I would have fought."

The history lived with him in a deeply emotional way even though he had never directly experienced racism in the music industry. "I'm not saying that there isn't any. But I think they [music executives] just knew not to do it around me. So maybe they are racist, but they were smart enough not to do it around me and my crew."

And while aside from the offensive experience at the basketball game, Irv hadn't heard many racist comments as a child, he had developed an early schema about how race drove segregation and impoverished the lives of so many people in communities such as the one in which he grew up. He drew a sharp distinction between the social costs of America's historical racism and the way he experienced it on the call. "I grew up in the hood. . . . Everyone was violent. But it wasn't racism because there were no White people there."

It's in the context of Irv's intense emotions around the history of racism in America, and his modest exposure to racist comments, that his conversation with the record executive came as such a shock.

Just as Irv finished confronting the racism and disrespect—two separate and deeply upsetting offenses—the *Elle* reporter called. You can hear the pain Irv felt—almost as if he pushed all the pent-up anger onto J.Lo. After calling her a "lying bitch," Irv told the reporter, "We made the records. She just did what we said. She don't know who the fuck she was talking about."

In one hour, while high, Irv had a deeply troubling conversation with a music-industry legend and then fielded a call from a reporter about Irv's most important collaborator. The conversation with the executive unearthed deep emotions. He then plunged into the interview despite not having a wealth of experience dealing with the press. "I was the executive. I wasn't the artist. So I would get interviewed few and far between. I wasn't well-versed on interview politics or whatever."

The situation required Irv to pivot from an environment he knew well, interacting with music executives, to one that he hardly knew at all, talking to reporters. On top of that, his emotions made it difficult for him to regulate his behavior. Irv faced two distinct challenges: first, he had to confront a deeply offensive comment; then he had to switch between environments that had very different norms and expectations. There aren't many ways to prepare for the first, but on the second many professions have recognized that intensive training can help mitigate the risk that Irv experienced.

People who thrive in dynamic environments have developed frameworks and tools to avoid impulsive actions and to help guide decision-making. That training draws on intuition and adds the kind of structure that prevents unthinking responses. To illustrate the alternative, it helps to consider first a context far removed from what Irv experienced. For example, fighter pilots rely on a system developed by

US Air Force Colonel John Boyd, who did everything from fly combat missions in the Korean War to advise Defense Secretary Dick Cheney during the first Gulf War.

Boyd lived through a period of tumultuous technological advances. Those changes dramatically altered the nature of a pilot's job and represented a profound shift in the nature of warfare. For centuries, armies fought fixed battles that depended on the size of their armies, the resilience of their supply chains, and the wisdom of their commanders.

In an aerial battle between two pilots flying faster than the speed of sound, advanced planning and careful logistical preparation mattered far less than the ability to adjust to rapidly changing conditions.

Boyd codified these new requirements in the acronym OODA: observe, orient, decide, act. He taught pilots that within seconds they had to observe their environment, orient themselves within it, decide on a strategy, then act on their decisions. Pilots used OODA to avoid the biases that might lead them to make bad decisions. The technique had such resonance that it got adapted in fields as diverse as litigation and consulting.[1]

There are lots of versions of OODA. Or, more accurately, lots of frameworks that help with decision-making.

Professor Kristina Guo devised a helpful acronym, DECIDE: D, determine the problem; E, establish the criteria; C, consider the alternatives; I, identify the choice; D, develop the plan of action; and E, evaluate the solution.[2]

Those work well for trained professionals. Most of us, however, need something simpler and easier to remember. Something that helps us slow down. One study of chess players found "that both experts and less skilled individuals benefit significantly from extra deliberation regardless of whether the problem is easy or difficult."[3]

The author Cheryl Strauss Einhorn has a clever expression based on the natural world that helps "put a speed bump in our thinking—a strategic stop to give us time to pause, to see the whole picture, and to reflect on what we're experiencing."[4]

She calls these strategic stops a "cheetah pause," as cheetahs have not only incredible speed, but also an amazing ability to decelerate. We all tend to rush after problems. Einhorn points out that a careful pause can help make that rushing much more effective. For relatively uncomplicated matters, it's as simple as not hitting Send on an angry email until you've thought about it overnight (e.g., remember David's email to Brad Pitt).

Tools such as OODA take repeated practice to become effective. They may also seem quaint amid emotionally charged conversations such as the one Irv experienced before the interview. Embracing simpler techniques, however, such as taking a cheetah pause (or just a deep breath) can help us regulate ourselves in stressful situations. It helps to remember Stephen Covey's quote, which he attributed to Viktor Frankl, "Between stimulus and response there is a space. In that space lies our power to choose our response, in our response lies our growth and our happiness."[5]

Irv did not take a cheetah pause. Instead, in the heat of the moment, he took his anger toward the record executive and hurled it at the *Elle* reporter. That's a classic example of displacement: the transference of one emotional reaction (fury toward the executive) onto another (the *Elle* reporter—or even J.Lo).

Irv didn't immediately realize that he had a problem. "When I got off the phone with *Elle* magazine, I thought nothing of it. It hit me when they sent me the transcripts of what they was gonna print." Did he try to stop its publication? "I gave it my effort. But after my effort, I just let it go."

At the time the *Elle* article came out, neither J.Lo nor the world knew about the call with the executive. All they knew was what they read. "Needless to say, it ruined my relationship with J.Lo. I apologized. I poured my heart out to her. I sent her candy and flowers and apologized a million times. 'You know, I was high. The fight with the executive. That's no excuse. I apologize.' And she accepted my apology. But it forever damaged that relationship. I should have never let my anger get the best of me and let it bleed onto J.Lo."

From his seat deep inside J.Lo's camp, Irv felt the chill immediately. "Superstars like J.Lo, they have a small circle of people who they could trust, and I think I was in there for a second. And I totally ruined it. That's one of the biggest things that I regret because she was just a beautiful, nice human being to me, and I did some dickhead shit."

Even his closest friends couldn't understand it. "They thought I was an idiot. They was laughing because they was like, 'Gotti, he's fucking crazy!' But no one was cool with it."

Irv owned it. "I'm an asshole for the J.Lo situation, totally in the wrong, and I'm a complete idiot. Make sure you say that—that I said that. I'm a complete idiot. She didn't warrant that. She didn't warrant nothing that I said. She was my friend."

Years later, when we interviewed him, Irv had not moved on. He didn't pretend that he didn't care about the loss. He was also able to separate what had happened with J.Lo from his conversation with the record executive.

As it relates to J.Lo, "I'm way different now. I would never do something like that again or run off and say damaging things to someone who I consider my friend. The mistakes that I've made would never, ever, ever happen again."

On racism, the fire had not diminished. "I like to stay with the Jewish community, right? So with the Jewish community, you can't play with that Holocaust shit. Their ancestors and their people suffered insurmountable fucking violent, dehumanizing things. You can't play with that. It's the same thing for N-words and Black people. We suffered in America, not human things. Raped, pillaged, everything . . . And that word personifies it."

Irv reconciled two thoughts: his desire to heal and to remember. He had even come to terms with the record executive. "He's a friend. He apologized the next time I'd seen him, 'Irv, you know, I didn't mean that. I would never be like that.' I just let it go and was like, 'Cool.' Never came up again. He's seen how mad I was. I think it was a learning lesson for him as well to not say or do that. So time heals all wounds. But I'll never forget it."

Irv had not lost the emotional connection to his childhood, which gave him a strong sense of independence. "You come from nothing—what's risky? If you don't do it, you're back to nothing. I had nothing before."

The reference to "coming from nothing" suggests one last aspect of why the whole situation felt so painful. Irv explained that coming from his neighborhood, having fought so hard for what he'd achieved, protecting that success takes on a particular importance. It's "entrenched with us, helping our families and the people that we love. So if you come along and you try to stop this success, oh, you're gonna have a problem."

Irv was clear about what happens to people who make that mistake. "You're gonna have a fucking big, big problem if you try and stop this flow and stop this success. I'm addicted to it. To this day, I'm addicted to taking care of my family, taking care of everybody: the nieces, the nephews, the grandbabies, my mom, and the grandkids."

12

It's Not Having What You Want; It's Wanting What You Have

Growing up in Soldotna, Alaska, Ann Mabeus had "lemonade stands starting when I was in third grade and just worked, worked, worked."

When she speaks about her childhood, she radiates pride. "Coming from families of teachers and also entrepreneurs—my dad had a fishing-guide service called Grand Slam Charters—we loved to be self-sufficient. Loved the independence!"

Thirty years after starting her own lemonade stand, she got conned by a "no risk, get rich quick" Ponzi scheme that rocked her religious community. To understand what happened, it helps to remember how far she had traveled. It's a real-life fish-out-of-water story. The kind you usually see in the movies and television series: *Beverly Hillbillies*, *Schitt's Creek*, and *Witness*.

If you wanted to locate a show about a family exiled from a big city to the "frontier," you could do worse than look around Kenai, Alaska.

South of the city, along the coast, there's Clam Gulch (population 209). A little farther down you'll find Happy Valley (population about 600). Up the Kenai River to the east, you pass through the town of Funny River (population nearly 1,000) on the way to Moose Pass (population 200 or so).

Then you wonder about all those Russian names: tiny towns such as Nikolaevsk, Razdolna, and Voznesenka, and bigger ones such as Soldotna, which means "soldier." Peter the Great hired the Danish cartographer Vitus Bering to explore the region in the 1700s. Hence, the Bering Strait, which separates Russia from Alaska, and all those Russian names.

Appropriately, the map still echoes with the history of the Indigenous people who preceded the Russians and the Europeans by so many, many years: Ninilchik and Cohoe. Oh, and Soldotna was actually probably named after the Dena'ina word "ts'eldat'nu," meaning "trickling down creek."

"I totally loved it," Ann says. "You feel like part of a community. You establish roots. I came from roots. I was born in a hospital two blocks down the street from my childhood home, which my parents still own."

She exudes the values that so many find missing in today's society: basic decency and hard work.

Decency: "When you're within that close-knit group, no matter what religion or group, when you spend a lot of time with people, you create these really deep-rooted friendships, relationships. You really rely on each other."

Hard work: "Loved to work, loved to make money, loved to think of new ways to make money."

As a girl and a young woman, Ann was a planner.

"I'd have a goal in mind." One summer, as a young girl, she wanted a mountain bike. "So I learned to save. And then, at the end of the summer, I bought it. I was really proud of that, and it just spurred my excitement and zest for real independence."

She left Alaska for the University of Arizona to study architecture, which she paid for with summer jobs cleaning fishing boats and bed-and-breakfasts. Then, right before she went back to school for her sophomore year, she got pregnant. She had only casually dated the father, a neighbor.

"I left for college, and I found out at ten weeks that I was pregnant, and it was a real big shock. I was away at school my whole entire pregnancy. I'm real tall. I'm five feet ten. So when I came back for Christmas, you couldn't tell I was pregnant." The baby came in April. The wedding in July.

It wasn't remotely a question about whether Ann would have her child. She grew up Catholic. Her faith mattered.

Ann remembers the wedding much less fondly than her baby. "I can't remember the food we had. I can't remember the flavor of the cake. I honestly didn't pick much out at all. My mom said the whole time, 'Are you sure you're doing this? Are you sure you're going through with this? Is it what you want?'"

"I just kept saying, 'Yes, yes, yes, it's what I want.' She said, 'I don't feel like you're very excited about this.' She called it out. . . . I did not want to disappoint anybody or have a child and not be wed. It was just like this was the best choice for everybody."

Step back a moment to form your mental image: A small-town woman grows up in a family of teachers who focus on religion, hard work coupled with thrift, and community. She follows those precepts, gets accepted to college out of state, and then suddenly finds herself married and with a baby.

If you imagined that this meant a life in Soldotna, guess again.

Twenty years after getting married, Ann lives in Henderson, Nevada—an affluent suburb of Las Vegas. For the first six years after her marriage, her husband played minor league baseball. After living in the same house for the first twenty-one years of her life, Ann went on to live in dozens over the next ten.

She embraced the life of a baseball player's wife while remaining focused on the financial impact of living on minor league salaries—the average player makes about $44,000 per year while constantly traveling. The marriage survived in no small part thanks to Ann's frugality.

In addition, her husband's religion—he's a member of the Church of Jesus Christ of Latter-day Saints (LDS)—played an important part in keeping them together. Ann did not convert at the time of her marriage. Rather, the pressures of a young marriage, her husband's itinerant life, and financial strain left the couple looking for new ways to bond.

"I just knew we were at a turning point. I thought for sure that we were going to get a divorce. Or I was going to have to try to be LDS." It wasn't a hard decision. While the marriage had its imperfections, Ann wanted to make it work and thought that a shared religion, and the community it would provide, would help make them closer.

When her husband's playing career ended, he began a series of sales jobs that utilized his outgoing personality and experience traveling to small cities. The work provided a growing sense of financial stability, but not the wealth that Ann had hoped his baseball career might have provided.

In the summer of 2019, Ann and her husband, as well as a group of other guests, got invited by a couple from their church on a trip to Mexico. They stayed in "this gorgeous, massive modern home that cost twenty-five thousand dollars for four or five days"; they flew down and back by "private jet"; sometimes they didn't go out to dinner so a chef could make "this big extravagant dinner."

One can almost hear echoes of Michael's description of the table read: precise memories of specific details—the observer can't quite believe her or his good fortune and has a strong desire to become part of the group.

On one of the first days, Ann overheard the host mention an investment opportunity. "I was just kind of picking up on bits and pieces." The man who pitched the idea was "very laid-back. He had absolutely perfected his craft, for sure. He was not really trying to do a sales pitch."

He described how he'd been fortunate enough to get the opportunity to invest in slip-and-fall accident claims. After just a quick explanation, Ann thought she understood the concept: someone gets into an accident, wins a claim, and wants access to the money before it gets paid. Investors pay the money to the claimant and then get paid back as soon as the lawsuit is settled.

The money goes to the claimant, interest gets paid on it—at quite an attractive rate—and then ninety days later the principal gets returned. Clear, quick, risk-free. Each claim gets fronted and settled separately, so even if one contract has a problem, it does not in any way undermine the certainty of the others.

Over the next couple of days, as the group lounged by the pool, they discussed it again and again. It turned out that many of Ann's neighbors and friends had either helped organize the investments or invested in them.

Ann's host made it sound so simple. He expressed such gratitude for the lifestyle these investments had afforded his family and him. Ann was thinking, "This might be a great opportunity."

"Knowing the [other families involved] and knowing them for years, I just felt comfortable with what they were involved in." Their host "was naming names. So I thought, 'They're doing it. I'm doing it.'"

One warning sign emerged that Ann only realized too late. "They told us we weren't allowed to contact the clients or anything like that. So we thought, 'Okay, confidentiality. That's fine.'"

Ann's primary concern related to her family's financial ability to participate, not the deal's legitimacy. She asked if they could start with a small investment. "He goes, 'You can really just start with whatever. Some people say one hundred thousand dollars. Some, you know, say sixty thousand dollars. Whatever.'"

By the time she left, Ann felt committed. "I opened up an LLC and a business bank account and got the ball rolling. I'm pretty sure we invested about one hundred thousand dollars right out of the gate." Ninety days later, they expected their first payment. "Sure enough, everything is fine."

Over the next two years, Ann's family invested over $900,000 (about half of their net worth), and for two years everything went well. They invested in new contracts, received their interest and principal, reinvested; and eventually, through a combination of interest and return of principal, they received back slightly more than they invested.

Not just that, they continued to invest so they had roughly a similar amount still at work: roughly $900,000 in, roughly $900,000 out, and about $900,000 still invested.

Alas, this financial "success" and the opportunity to settle in a community could not overcome the troubles in her marriage. By early 2023, having recently divorced, Ann began pondering her next step as a single mother of four children. She discussed it with friends and family over coffee and meals. Most of the conversations have faded from her memory. But one stands out.

Ann remembers sitting in a Starbucks as she advised a friend about private school admissions strategies. Outside the window, she watched as numerous police vehicles streamed by headed toward her neighborhood. Suddenly, her phone rang. One of her neighbors breathlessly reported that FBI agents had raided another neighbor's home. Her friend asked Ann if she was involved in the "investment" that the raided neighbor had promoted.

"Not really," Ann replied, because she didn't invest with that particular neighbor. She invested through someone else. It quickly became clear that the FBI had raided multiple homes, including those of the very people who had recruited Ann and her husband into the scheme.

Within a day, as rumors swirled and press coverage started, Ann began to fear that her $900,000 investment had disappeared. She held out hope that because the FBI had not raided the homes of some of the people from that Mexico trip, she might escape unscathed.

She reached out to them. First over the phone, because a written exchange seemed unwise given the raids. Then, when she got no response, she texted: "Hey, we need to talk. I really need to speak with you." Again, no response.

Finally, after a few days, her contact promised to set up calls for the end of the week, when he would explain the situation. Days went by, leaving Ann in exquisite agony. When she finally spoke to him, he was worse than no help. "He goes, 'This is such a tragedy. I don't know what to think about it. We're all victims in this, you know?' Just kind of la la la."

Even though Ann had put down a retainer for an attorney, she still wanted to believe that "he's a good person. He'll take care of it." Her confidence was misplaced. There were no slip-and-fall contracts; no escrow accounts or interest payments. Just fraud. An old-fashioned, carefully executed Ponzi scheme.

Suddenly, a woman who had prided herself on her financial prudence and independence found herself in a terrible spot. When she got divorced, she agreed to receive alimony for only a limited time since she thought she could count on regular interest payments from the investment in the Ponzi scheme.

Not only had Ann lost access to her investment and stopped receiving the interest payments, but she also needed to worry about "claw back" payments because she had actually received back slightly more from the Ponzi scheme than she'd invested. She knew that the authorities might claim that she had "made" money on the scheme even though Ann would not get back the $900,000 that she thought she was owed. How had she let this happen and how would she get back on her feet?

Imagine that you saw a picture of Ann and her friends lounging by the pool in Mexico. Could you identify Ann just by her expression? By virtue of their socioeconomic, geographic, and religious backgrounds, would some of the guests have looked more comfortable than others? Would some appear more deeply part of that momentary community?

For an outsider, it would likely prove impossible. For a member of that community, it would probably appear obvious. Ann knew she wanted to belong. She just couldn't see herself or the situation clearly.

It's hard for people to know themselves. So hard that most animals can't even recognize themselves. In 1970, the psychologist Gordon Gallup Jr. (not the Gallup who founded the polling organization) devised the mirror test to determine self-awareness in animals. In the test, animals got exposed to a mirror. Then, after they acclimated to its presence, they had a colored sticker or dye placed on their head.

Those animals that investigated the mark on their head, rather than thinking that the reflection was another animal, "passed" the test.[1] Only humans, great apes, bottlenose dolphins, elephants, and magpies can do it.

While those few animals can see themselves, humans take it one step further: we tend to see echoes of ourselves even when we're not in the picture.

Imagine showing two of your friends a photograph of a large family having dinner. In the photo, some of the family members are laughing, some look concerned, some stare at their phones.

One of your friends thinks that the family looks dysfunctional: they're having separate conversations, their emotions differ, some seem checked out. Your other friend reacts quite differently. She thinks the interaction looks great: spirited, individualistic, and fun.

Same photo, two very different reactions. Why? Because we bring to every situation our own experiences and intuitions. In the case of the dinner photo, it's possible that your friends had very different types of family dinners growing up. Or maybe they've lived through a series of painful dinners with their in-laws. Or maybe one of your friends is generally more optimistic, the other prone to depression. Their schemas and emotions mean that they react very differently to the same photo.

Ann saw the group of people lounging around the pool in Mexico and wanted to believe that she had found her place in a financially successful community. She inserted herself into the "photo." After all the years wandering through small minor league baseball towns, after managing on her husband's modest income, she finally saw a path to achieving her economic and social ambitions.

The first months after learning about the fraud didn't provide any room for reflection.

"I am spiraling. I have no money. I'm a disaster. I can't sleep. I can't eat. I lose twelve pounds in a week, which is rare for me, which is amazing. Actually, let's do that again!" She smiles as she recounts a terrible period in her life and then the humor fades quickly.

"[I became] a prisoner in my own home because I didn't want to spend any money. I didn't want to eat because then I would have to buy more groceries. I had to go back to court to get some emergency money from my ex-husband."

She wanted to regain her childhood independence and work ethic. After thirteen years as a stay-at-home mom, she began the search for a new job. She didn't want to teach—her previous profession—"because

I wasn't going to be able to survive on about forty-eight grand a year. There's just no way."

At many corporate interviews, she heard the same thing: "'We love your personality, go get a job somewhere else for a year, and then come back to us.' I was going to be homeless by then." When she applied to other jobs, she'd "make it for four rounds out of five interviews, and then would just be exhausted. It was so much time wasted."

Her situation grew more and more dire. "My dad's paying my rent. My aunt's paying for my car." She hated relying on others. "I have to be self-sufficient."

Finally, she came to an agreement with her ex-husband, found a job as a real estate agent, and slowly began to take control of her life. She worried, "but as far as the anger goes, I just don't have time for it."

With a modicum of normalcy restored to her life, she began to unpack why she and her husband had fallen for the fraud. Her first thought goes to her lack of due diligence. Aside from a cursory conversation with their CPA, they had not investigated the investment at all. They had relied on her conversations in the pool and the fact that they knew so many other participants. Full stop. Ann doesn't dwell on it partly because she takes ultimate responsibility for the family's finances.

"I was the family CFO. I was good at taking care of money for the most part, until this situation." Her husband deferred to her because while her childhood had stability and financial planning, his had far less of both. "He knew me growing up. I think you're mostly a product of your environment."

Ann's reliance on the values she'd learned as a child meant two things. First, when she felt comfortable about a situation, she "hyper-speeded" her research—that's a slightly generous way of saying that she didn't seriously review the investment. Second, having seen how her environment shaped her, she focused on the people with whom she invested. Growing up, she formed a schema that she could trust people in her tight community.

Originally, that meant the people in Soldotna. Then, after she got married, she relied increasingly on members of her new faith. Leaving aside the much more important aspects of how religion affected her family and her, the new religious community proved to have a profound impact on her investment decision-making.

First, the people who invited her on the trip to Mexico and offered her a chance to invest belonged to her church.

Second, her CPA belonged to the church.

Third, many of the other perpetrators and victims did as well. She started investing partly because her partners were "all members of the church." Her schema made it hard to separate the bad actors from the hardworking, decent people who made up the vast majority of her religious community.

The reference to "members" gives a window into another set of the warning signs that Ann missed. The perpetrators of the fraud used almost all of the classic techniques of playing into their victims' desire for membership in an elite, prosperous club.

They started with the soft sell while around the swimming pool.

Then they emphasized their social and religious connections, which gave them credibility and status.

They targeted people who wanted to be part of their financial world and who would hesitate to ask too many questions given those connections. As Ann says about herself, "I don't like to disappoint people or burn bridges." The word "disappoint" echoes exactly why she decided to get married quickly.

The investment itself was just simple enough to be understood, but sufficiently complex that it proved hard to perform due diligence. The perpetrators compounded that effect by preventing contact with the clients.

The investment had seemingly "guaranteed" returns that paid out regularly, coupled with "low" risk.

Finally, as the fraudsters became more and more dependent on new victims to pay back the early investors, they increased the pressure.

In the beginning, they were "laid-back and 'beachy' with no pressure or anything." Then, in the months leading up to the FBI raids, the pressure increased. Ann heard from them regularly: "Hey, guys, we really need more investors. If you have friends interested, get them to me. Give me their contact information. We have so many clients and contracts that we can't fill. . . . If we can't fill the clients in contracts, you know, we're not going to be able to get business from these law firms."

She saw the change. "I mean it really took like a one-eighty. And I was like, 'Gosh, this is so pushy.'" Yet, the community ties deadened her antennae.

So many people fall victim to Ponzi schemes that Ann's decision to invest hardly seems remarkable. That's especially true given how many people in her own community made the same decision. That she took such reassurance from participation by others in her community, however, suggests a more complicated set of underlying dynamics.

Having grown up with incredible stability, her life changed dramatically in her twenties. First because of an unexpected child, then a rushed marriage, and then many years of an itinerant existence driven by her husband's baseball ambitions. By the time she decided to invest in the Ponzi scheme, she had finally begun to reclaim the stability and financial safety that she'd cherished as a child. She wanted to accelerate that reclamation, plus she felt at least some aspiration for the lifestyle she witnessed in Mexico. "It was like maybe we could recover some of the money lost when [my husband] played baseball."

The investment also clearly made her feel closer to her LDS neighbors and friends. "Everybody I knew was LDS. I just felt like it was nice that we were hand-selected to be involved with this."

Compare that to the way she describes Soldotna. "You just love each other, and you help each other, and they are some of my closest friends still to this day." She had a schema about friendship and community formed during a stable childhood. Trust and financial security went together.

Ann reveals the complexity of her self-perception. She has firmly held schemas about community and financial security that got shaped throughout her childhood. She also, like many of us, had deeply held convictions that ran up against the reality of life. Before she separated from her husband, she "didn't believe in divorces—like just better-together type of thing. I don't have anybody in my huge family—nobody's divorced. That really wasn't an option."

The woman who said, "I don't like when there's business and friendship that overlaps because I feel like those lines get blurred sometimes," invested with her neighbors and friends.

Someone who prided herself on the kind of grinding, methodical work that characterized her early years, then allocated half her family's net worth in an investment that "was going to *catapult* us back into where we should have been to begin with." A scheme that offered fast riches instead of fair pay for hard work.

Those contradictions make her decision more understandable: she wanted her family to have financial stability; she tried to assimilate into a new religious community; and she still believed in what she had learned as a child. What this doesn't explain, however, is her persistent optimism.

It bothers her that some of the perpetrators have continued to live their lives—at least for the moment—unburdened by any legal consequences. "The thing that makes me ill, I would say, like really, genuinely makes my stomach turn is the fact that they are walking around town. Their kids are wearing nice clothes. They're living in one of their homes that they bought with *our* money. It makes me sick, but it's not anger.

"I just don't have time to be so angry because I have to make progress, so let justice fall where it may. . . . I really didn't want to be vengeful." Nor does she blame others for her decision. She reflects on the three most momentous events in her life: her first pregnancy, her marriage, and the decision to make this investment.

"I never really made the decision to have kids early. That was a surprise. I did make the decision to get married because I felt like it was the right choice. I definitely did make the decision to invest in this investment." Of the three decisions, only her children give her joy.

The economic uncertainty, however, hurts, as does the loss of trust. "Now, I'm a little less trusting. I was very trusting. Loved people, loved relationships, loved connecting with other people."

She lives thousands of miles away from her childhood community, but an even further distance from its ethos. "It doesn't feel good because I feel like character and integrity are huge. You have good examples that you grew up with, and I think that you want to replicate those."

She believes "work hard, invest, live within your means. It's not that difficult. This was a constant since we were in high school. And I know where I come from." The problem is that she no longer lives in Soldotna. So many of her values, and so much of the strength that she derived from them, have survived the hot Nevada desert, yet it's almost impossible to live within the glare of the Vegas Strip and not have it permeate at least some decision-making and distort some of what she learned as a girl.

13

Portrait of an Artist as a Young Man

Michael Govan's everyday work uniform—dark tailored suit, white shirt, and understated tie—resembles that of a stylish Swiss banker, but when he speaks with his customary intelligence on art, culture, and science, he sounds like an academic or even a conceptual artist. In fact, he's the director and CEO of the Los Angeles County Museum of Art. He does not like it when people try to categorize him or his profession. "We're category seekers, especially since the nineteenth century; we have to put things in a box and that changes how we think."

That unwillingness to conform to labels began during his undergraduate years at Williams College. "My problem was I was against categories." So, he tried his hand at journalism, and long before most people had access to a computer, let alone programmed one, Michael "was a computer programmer programming artificial intelligence." A good one too. "I could be an art patron if I had followed that course." In some circles, "art patron" means really, really wealthy. Tech entrepreneurs who went to college in the early eighties did just fine; Jeff Bezos, born a few months after Michael, comes to mind.

He moved from discipline to discipline with ease, excelling at all of them. His group of friends did not fall into a specific group or clique. As he describes it, "I inhabited all these different worlds with different networks."

Yet, over and over he reverted back to art, partly because it eluded oversimplification. He studied art history, created it as an artist, and even, at the age of twenty-three, curated an exhibit at the Williams College Museum of Art, one of the country's most prestigious college museums. As an undergraduate, he had taken so many graduate-level courses that he considered getting a graduate degree in art history.

Upon graduation, he weighed pursuing his technology interests or continuing down the path as a curator. He decided to work as a curator for two years at the Williams College Museum, overseeing art programs and the building of new galleries. He also helped launch a new museum project in the nearby depressed former factory town of North Adams, which eventually opened as MASS MoCA (Massachusetts Museum of Contemporary Art). Then he walked away from it all to take a full scholarship to study art—not art history—at the University of California, San Diego.

He describes the decision more in the language of a curator than an artist. "I could go there [art school] and I would have access to all these ideas: environmental, technological, and the cultural shifts [that represented] the seeds of decolonization and feminism."

Years before these issues became embedded on university campuses, Michael saw how they related to his work. "All of that was deeply embedded in the art world before a lot of other fields." While in graduate school, Michael loved learning under the tutelage of Allan Kaprow, a man Michael describes as a "progenitor of performance art and conceptual art in the sixties." In addition, Michael worked with a range of scholars and artists including David Antin, an extraordinary poet, writer, artist, and art critic, and his wife, Eleanor Antin, an influential performance artist and filmmaker. Michael surrounded himself with serious, innovative artists—the ideal environment for a student at the start of his career.

In the midst of his studies, Tom Krens, Michael's old boss at the Williams Museum and newly appointed director at the Guggenheim Museum in New York City, invited Michael to join him as his deputy. Krens sat atop a modest bureaucracy that wielded disproportionate influence in the art world. He attracted brilliant curators (the museum administrators who oversaw specific collections and mounted exhibits) while becoming one of the first museum leaders to seduce donors and corporations in a determined effort to restore an institution that had declined—financially and artistically—since Frank Lloyd Wright designed its home. The Guggenheim was about to go through a massive transformation, and Krens needed help.

Krens, Michael says, "insisted I come and made the argument that I could finish school later." And Kaprow, Michael's graduate school mentor, endorsed the decision; Kaprow thought of programming the Guggenheim space as a form of performance art. While the interruption might have made some artists uncomfortable, Michael could immediately see the advantages.

Worst case: "I figured I would learn something that would help forge my course in art, which I fully felt I would go back to after a few years. I was a hundred percent committed [to life as an artist], so it was like taking time off for something like the Peace Corps." Albeit an assignment on Fifth Avenue in New York City.

He felt as if he could add museum administrator to his life as an artist: an "and" decision rather than an "or" choice. In fact, working for the Guggenheim at that moment represented a very specific approach to the art world. The Guggenheim, unlike the Metropolitan Museum of Art, worked mostly with living artists who had achieved sufficient recognition and success to merit an exhibition in the Guggenheim's circular halls.

Michael wanted to work with living artists, but that didn't drive the decision. If it had, he could have worked for a major contemporary art gallery. That path would have allowed him to help propel those artists to wider recognition while also potentially making Michael extraordinarily wealthy. Again, just as when he had passed up the technology world, money did not seem to play a role in his decision. Instead, he chose the quasi-academic path of museum curatorship.

More important, he thought he could combine his administrative duties and the creation of art. "I, at that time, thought about how Paul Gauguin was a stockbroker until he was thirty-five. And Wallace Stevens was an insurance executive while he wrote poetry. Leonardo da Vinci is a perfect case in point. He was an engineer as well."

Michael's young age influenced his decision. "The cult of artists is that they break out in their twenties, and they're young emerging artists and people really love the things they did early. But if you really study artists and artwork, so much of what we call great art is from older people."

Michael persuaded himself that he could live in both worlds even if the actual creation of art would have to wait. He felt he could have a "foot in and a foot out"—with the definition of "in" and "out" left ambiguous. Ambiguity appealed to his antipathy toward categorizing himself and ideas along rigid lines.

The aspiration of "artist as executive" ran into the hard wall of an incredibly demanding job. Within two years of joining the Guggenheim, Michael had stopped making art and would not do it again. His rapid career progression had simply consumed all his art-making creativity and time.

He considers the decision to give up his career as an artist as the biggest mistake of his life: "It was a giant fork in the road, and, to this day, I question it just because I'm wearing a tie."

That tie, along with the elegant dark suit that has come to define his personal style, became the symbol of the transition away from his academic UCSD colleagues. Working as a curator put him into a precarious position with the artists who'd supervised his work as a student.

"What did Allan Kaprow and all those accomplished artists want? They wanted to show at the Guggenheim. I wasn't an assistant. I wasn't a consultant doing graphic design. I was in the central administration of decisions of a major museum. It was a giant conflict of interest. I had to go one way or the other."

It wasn't just that conflict that kept Michael away from his art. "I was traveling to Tokyo for a day or Moscow for a few days. Maybe it was like a drug, the energy?" Museum curators lead, by necessity, frenetic lives: raising money from temperamental donors, browbeating museum directors and art collectors to secure pieces for upcoming exhibitions, visiting with artists in their remote studios. It's all-consuming.

Artists lead different lives. "I mean, to be an artist, you have to be fairly solitary. I think that you have to perfect a craft. The repetitive obsessive quality protects you from other influences that will screw up your receptors.

"[As an artist] your sensory antennae are more raw and exposed; [because] of isolation you feel things with more sensitivity. [But] to work in the center of business, you have to close off your senses for survival." Or, at least, attune those antennae to different frequencies— the needs of employees and donors.

While Michael cites the artists who combined commercial lives with their artistic ones and knows that others lead jet-setting lives that resemble those of museum directors (e.g., Jeff Koons), he has a different mental image of himself as an artist.

"I have no illusions that I would have become a famous artist. That has nothing to do with it. I might have been an artist teacher. I didn't imagine myself an important gallery artist who made a lot of money in conceptual art anyway. But it's a difference of a creative life and a thoughtful life and how you contribute and have breakthroughs of thought depending on how you spend your day."

He carried two conflicting schemas: one for a successful artist, the other for a responsible adult. Having studied with highly influential and commercially underappreciated professors at UCSD, he thought the creative process required relative isolation. His schema for an "artist" conflicted with how some of the artists on display at the Guggenheim socialized with collectors and other influential members of the establishment. Many of those artists had ambitions that ran beyond recognition of their work. They wanted their work to sell.

Michael's schema for a successful artist, one that prioritized making meaningful contributions and disregarded financial success, ran into conflict with his schema about being a responsible adult. From an early age, as evidenced by what he accomplished in college, he took on "ridiculous responsibilities." His ability and desire to become the curator and deputy director at a major museum at the age of twenty-six and then assume even greater responsibilities shortly thereafter came partly from what he'd witnessed as a child.

Michael's mother always worked. "After graduate school in political science she was a teacher and an activist. She had five jobs. She went back to get her law degree at Georgetown night school while working full-time. I saw all that struggle at that time." Michael knew that other families had mothers who drove them around and provided more day-to-day support, but "our family didn't work that way. Of course, I thought it's genius and thank God my mother didn't dote over me. She loved me without having much time, which gave me this freedom."

He admired his mother's career while internalizing how it caused tension and uncertainty for family life. He also spent most of his extracurricular time going to protests and county board meetings and getting petitions signed instead of hanging out with friends his age. He recalls occasional death-threat calls to their family home because of their family's efforts to promote mass transit and stop a planned eight-lane interstate highway that would destroy neighborhoods. Witnessing the stress that put on his parents' lives and relationship caused Michael to grow up quickly. He felt that he had to help keep everyone together. He learned a lot about conflict and honed his diplomatic skills in this environment.

"Through my entire high school and college, I was the adult by far. In high school, and during the first week of college, we had all these wild kids who would set off the fire alarms and get read the riot act. I negotiated our way out of it because I knew one of the deans and was able to communicate the situation. So I was a bit of a parent in my college dorm. I didn't go to a lot of parties, didn't have that many wild experiences as a kid. Because of that, I never took drugs. Because the world was too serious."

Adulthood meant acting "seriously," and the Guggenheim job just felt more "serious" than an artist's life. His flirtation with conceptual art ended quickly after he had the chance to become a "true" adult with the travel, recognition, and opportunity that the job provided.

The choice felt binary. "And now people always say, 'Oh, do you still make art? Are you an artist?' And I say, 'No.' It's not because I can't draw—I can tell you exactly the mechanisms; I can make art that looks like art, especially the conceptual art that I pursued. I know how to do that, but the sensory apparatus has changed so much."

Today, Michael just doesn't feel that he has the option for that kind of openness. "I've had more people in my office in emotional distress this year than any year in the past. I'm not allowed to break down or show any signs of stress because people will read it."

He feels that he needs to maintain that emotional reserve to operate effectively. Successful leaders have different approaches to how they interact with their employees and other constituents. Michael tries to keep some separation from the world around him. Without at least some barrier between his job and his personal life, it would become overwhelming.

Contrast that necessary separation with his perspective on artists, who, he thinks, have far greater permeability between the world and their work. They "have to develop an entirely different sensory apparatus and then convert your whatever you want to call it—new ideas, radical ideas, turning things around you—you have to convert them into a different way of thinking and deploying that energy from the side. I don't really see how I could go back."

His art-making antennae had withered. He misses that ability to feel more deeply, and the capacity to express those feelings through art. He's become that adult who both keeps down five jobs and tries to care for others.

Ultimately, though, his regret about the decision seems less about the decision than about his having made a choice at all. For someone who is committed to the idea that life and art should not fit into neat categories, the concept that he committed to a particular course so early in his life sits uneasily. While he knows that in today's art world "we live in categories of disciplines; we live in categories of choices," he has spent his professional life fighting against that propensity.

Wouldn't it be great if when faced with a decision we could try one option and then pivot to the other if we don't like the outcome? Or, better yet, enjoy both. Yogi Berra's advice resonates: "When you come to a fork in the road, take it."

In 1986, Drs. Markus and Nurius published a seminal paper in *American Psychologist* about the concept of possible selves. They argued that possible selves "represent individuals' ideas of what they might become, what they would like to become, and what they are afraid of becoming."[1]

Possible selves are forms of identity that capture a whole series of hopes and fears as well as aspirations; these possible selves extend beyond career to include relationships, family, material success, hobbies, and myriad other characteristics that define our lives.

When we make choices, we close doors on those possible selves. We give up childhood dreams, take jobs that seem boring but pay better, enter relationships because of our age. Remember Andy Davis, the young boy in *Toy Story* who loved both Buzz Lightyear and Woody. Andy imagined himself as either—or, better yet, both. Youth prevented him from having to choose.

In 1995, Professors Gilovich and Medvec published research that showed that in the short term, people have more regret about things they've done, but in the long term, inactions (things they didn't do) prove more painful.[2]

While we associate many of our most unpleasant memories with regretful actions—the hurtful comment, the foolish risk, the impulsive action—we have the opportunity to correct those through ameliorative actions. We can apologize, repair, and heal. We can't, however, take the other fork in the road.

In 2018, Professors Davidai and Gilovich published a new study focused on the connection between regret and different types of goals.[3] When asked to name their single biggest regret in life, like Michael, 76 percent of their study participants described not fulfilling an "ideal" goal (a dream or an aspiration, an ideal version of who they want to be), while 24 percent described not fulfilling an "ought" goal (a duty or responsibility, a version of themselves they feel they should be). Participants also reported more pain and regret about not fulfilling their hopes and aspirations than for not fulfilling their obligations and responsibilities.

People who focus on their "ideal" selves—the people they "wish" to be—can feel the pain particularly acutely. Much more acutely than people who focus on the "ought" selves—the people they "should" be.

Remember when Hillary Clinton said, "Shoulda, coulda, woulda"? Mistakes about "shoulda"—things we ought to do—don't feel nearly as intense as the "coulda" ones—things we wished we had done. Put differently, if you change Marlon Brando's line in *On the Waterfront* from "I coulda been a contender" to "I shoulda . . . ," it doesn't feel nearly as tragic.

Michael's desire to avoid categorization fits with how many people start their careers. Even if they stop fantasizing about unrealistic goals, they do not shed all their "possible selves."

Michael had good reason to have a long list of possible selves; by the end of college, he had already demonstrated aptitude across a wide swath of disciplines. As a result, giving them up likely generates more discomfort for him than for most of us whose fantasies have no bearing on reality—many people play little league, few make it to the major leagues.

He didn't give up a fantasy; he decided to forgo a real possibility. Michael fundamentally regrets giving up on one of his possible selves: Michael as a serious artist—the kind of artist who Michael the curator would respect. His current responsibilities, including the deeply public nature of running a museum, highlight the choice, as they contrast so sharply with how he thinks that most influential artists preserve their creativity.

His strategic and outward drive have clearly generated dividends. The new museum building project that he has championed for over a decade could almost certainly not have happened without his relentless fundraising and political mobilization. It's generated enormous enthusiasm in some quarters and intense public criticism from select journalists and community members. All done out in the open.

In important ways, he has preserved his devotion to embracing complexity and dismissing overly rigid categories. He has filled his life with contradictions and possibilities.

"The notion of a mistake is so complex. It actually revealed, for me, a philosophy that I have, which is of my multiplicity of thinking, my multiculturalism, which is the way I run my museum and plan the future, with a view that all things are possible and there is a simultaneity of all possibilities and forks in the road."

The museum has taken on an institutional version of what he had hoped for his own career. "I'm driving my entire museum and decolonizing art history by putting everything on the same plane. . . . There are just so many possibilities and I see forks everywhere in decision-making, in the world."

We think of institutions as having such rigidity, yet in some cases they provide more flexibility than individual careers. Maintaining the possibility of "forks" in the road—keeping your options open—appeals to all of us. Giving up optionality, even when the choice leads to a positive outcome, causes regret.

Professors Davidai and Gilovich identified these issues so clearly that they titled one of their papers "The Ideal Road Not Taken: The Self-Discrepancies Involved in People's Most Enduring Regrets." Michael's decision has stayed painful partly because of the road not taken, but also because of the fundamental respect he has for artists who may represent an "ideal" version of himself.

Despite his desire to apply the principles of his early conceptual art to an institutional setting, Michael just doesn't have the same room to maneuver. While he would have liked to maintain a more fluid lens, the world required him to pick a path. Rather than maintaining a multitude of interests, identities, professions, and potential outcomes, Michael focused on one. When he came to the fork in the road, he made a choice. By all outward measures, he made the right one. Yet by succumbing to the world's demand for categories, the choice now feels like the mistake of his life.

14

If You Break It, You Own It

In 2018, nineteen years out of college, Liz Jenkins became CFO of Hello Sunshine, Reese Witherspoon's hot new production company. For an ex-consultant, former banker, and General Electric (GE) alumna, it was a dream job.

Despite Liz's pristine résumé, Witherspoon had taken a risk on her. Unlike Liz's previous corporate experiences, where she had a large finance infrastructure around her, at Hello Sunshine she had to build an entire team—including for functions where she had demonstrably less experience. Every company is different, but in general, CFOs worry about budgets (Liz had experience), strategy and financing (lots of experience), and accounting (not much at all).

If you don't come from the world of corporate finance, that can seem like a distinction without a difference, but Liz understood the importance. "I came from a background of investment banking and more corporate finance. Very early on in my career, I did internal audit at GE. But I'm not an accountant by any means. Not a CPA."

She had worked on acquisitions, formed strategic partnerships, and built budgets; she did not, however, have experience getting bills paid or balancing the books, the nitty-gritty work every company needs to make sure it can pass an audit and prevent fraud.

"The first person you hire as the CFO when you have zero team members is your controller." Controllers do all the bookkeeping; she wanted an accountant since that represented "my soft underbelly and my biggest vulnerability."

Liz got to work recruiting all-stars and wanted to get it right. "Hiring always matters. People always matter, but especially when you've got something in its infancy. . . . There's a lot of risk to making the wrong choice."

She thought she knew what she needed: someone with real experience who would bring credibility and demonstrate Liz's capacity to build a serious team. She may not have known double-entry bookkeeping, but she did know the playbook for hiring great people.

So Liz wrote a job description, hired a headhunter, and sent the word out to her personal network. So far so good. After interviewing lots of people, she identified two candidates: "One person who had a rather lengthy résumé that was almost overkill for a company of our size." And another who had a less lengthy résumé, but felt like a better cultural fit in personality and experience. She then did a whole series of careful interviews and reference checks on both.

Happily, she was in the land of good choices. Both of them checked a lot of boxes. She made the offer to the woman with more experience and persuaded her to accept it. "I did it," Liz thought. "That's great. Excellent! Yeah! Gold star for Liz." Liz's new colleagues applauded her decisiveness.

Having made the decision, "I felt a lot of relief because . . . the first thing that was, to me, the most critical piece to this component to my success in this role was done. So I felt great about it. . . . I felt confident in the decision."

It didn't take her long to realize that she had blown it. "There was just something that felt like a kind of niggling doubt. . . . I just knew. I knew that this person did not have that ability to function in this type of environment. . . . You can tell when it's like a lawn mower that's not turning over."

Despite her concerns, Liz focused on how to help her new hire succeed. Liz owned it. "I've got to figure out how to get this person's feet under them. I've made this choice. So how do I make this person feel comfortable?"

Liz recognized that the woman felt overwhelmed in an entrepreneurial environment that lacked structure and had such diverse responsibilities. Liz had a solution. "Let's simplify, simplify, simplify. Instead of these ten things, let's focus on this one thing." She then tried to re-create the classic corporate structure. Even simplified and restructured, it didn't work.

Two weeks later, Liz fired her. The woman reacted with "relief and then sadness for disappointing me, in letting me down."

Liz's first big decision was a monumental mistake. She felt so embarrassed. "It was really hard. That kept me up at night." Why would she have made a mistake so obvious that it became clear to her within days of having made it?

Here's the thing about the entertainment industry: It doesn't have much interest in pedigree. Many of the best agents started in the mail room; most of the talent didn't attend college. Liz quickly intuited that she had overly prioritized technical expertise. While Liz thought she needed someone with *deep* accounting experience, she actually needed someone who had *enough* accounting experience and could fit into the culture. She went back to the runner-up—who became a great success.

In Liz's description of the process, a few words serve as warning signs.

First, while Liz thought she knew what she needed in the candidates, her use of words such as "soft underbelly" and "vulnerability" to describe her experience suggest a level of unwarranted professional anxiety. She had the right list of strengths and weaknesses. Yet, she exaggerated her deficits, leading to a strong emotional reaction that overly influenced her decision. "So I'm down to these two candidates and . . . made a decision . . . really kind of out of fear with the concerns that I had about my own abilities."

That's affect bias: allowing our emotions to overly influence our rational decision-making. In analyzing her own work experience so deeply, she may have triggered an exaggerated emotional reaction—e.g., fear of not having the "right" skills to be a CFO. It may have made her overprioritize finding someone who had skills that she didn't.

Not just anyone; she hired someone who was "almost overkill for a company of our size." Someone who had the right "accreditations" as well. Accreditations certainly make sense if you're hiring a CPA—that's a licensed profession. Liz's word choice suggests a deeper connotation—someone who had the right pedigree. Someone like Liz who had had all the right jobs.

Many Black women have to work harder and make better decisions than their peers to achieve equal success. Given that phenomenon, and Liz's impeccable educational pedigree and GE experience, her focus on credentials made sense. They collectively gave her a deeply developed schema about hiring talent: focus on their credentials. Our first serious jobs out of college often have an outsize impact on how we view the world. That was certainly true in Liz's case. Given how GE has shrunk in size and importance, it's hard to remember the role it played in American business or the way it deeply shaped the careers of people such as Liz.

GE once had a reputation for attracting and developing great people. Jack Welch, the former CEO, famously spent a huge amount of time writing personal thank-you notes to team members and even more time firing underperformers.

Former executives at GE went on to become CEOs of Boeing, Home Depot, Albertsons, Honeywell, and 3M. Not all of them had success, but that didn't prevent corporate America from hiring GE alumni who had survived the gristmill. That's partly because of what they learned and partly because of the toughness they developed.

GE trained thousands of managers in everything from purchasing to manufacturing excellence to financial analysis. Before the whole thing went sideways, getting a job at GE put you on a path to corporate success—especially if you wanted to go into an analytically intense environment. At GE you learned to measure everything and assess everything through their fabled Six Sigma process.

From GE, Liz went on to the Wharton School—another desirable business credential with high expectations. Then, after a brief experience at McKinsey, the gold standard of consulting, she went into investment banking, where she felt "you're paid to be perfect. And you're paid to be right. The reason you get paid what you get paid is that you are very precise and really care about the details."

Between GE, Wharton, McKinsey, and Credit Suisse (the then-successful bank), she had close to a perfect financial pedigree. She felt ready for her next adventure: the entertainment industry—a field where she could begin to move away from the numbers, work with more creative people, and get out to Los Angeles. Working first as a strategist at MRC Studios, Liz learned the industry and took on more and more responsibility.

By the time she arrived at Hello Sunshine, Liz had racked up a decade of getting it right. In job after job, she had proven her analytical ability, the key skill she had learned at GE.

The candidate she chose conformed to the kind of person she expected to have in this role. She knew what had made her successful and applied the same standard to her candidates.

Liz likely used a "representativeness" heuristic: a mental shortcut where people make decisions based on how well something fits a prototype rather than on objective information.

In a classic study of the representativeness heuristic, Nobel Prize winner and Princeton professor Daniel Kahneman and his longtime collaborator Amos Tversky, a Stanford professor, conducted a study in three parts. First, they asked a group (the base-rate group) to estimate the percentage of total graduate students in each of several fields (e.g., business, computer science, engineering, humanities/education, medicine).

They then gave two groups a description of Tom W., a fictional graduate student: someone "of high intelligence . . . [with] a need for order and clarity . . . rather dull and mechanical . . . [and someone who] does not enjoy interacting with others."

Next, they asked the second group (the similarity group) to rank how similar Tom W. seemed to the typical graduate student in each field.

Finally, they asked the third group (the prediction group) to guess the likelihood that Tom was in each field. Based on the odds from the base-rate group, Tom W. was three times more likely to be a humanities or education major, but 95 percent of the prediction group ranked Tom W. as more likely to study computer science than humanities or education. The third group based their ratings on the similarity between Tom W. and their prototype of a computer science student. Put differently, they overweighted the similarity aspects and underweighted the base rates.[1]

A year later, in "Judgment under Uncertainty: Heuristics and Biases,"[2] Tversky and Kahneman described how a broader group of heuristics—or mental shortcuts—can lead us astray. Our schemas can compound the problem of mental shortcuts. In Liz's case, she used a mental prototype of how a controller should appear on paper and chose based on how well each candidate fit that image rather than using all of the information that she had on her company and the candidates. She used a shortcut that cut out valuable data points.

That prototype might have worked well at large companies such as GE and Credit Suisse—institutions that built their cultures and structures over more than a hundred years. Hello Sunshine had dozens of people and had basically only just opened. In that context, what appeared safe and responsible didn't fit with what the company actually needed.

Liz recognizes how her heuristics and schemas might have influenced her decision-making: in high-stakes situations, she tends to become more conservative in her choices. It's helpful here to associate the word "conservative" with "conventional"—she ran a textbook hiring process that resulted in a central-casting candidate. Liz wanted a "conservative" candidate who appeared safe and reduced Liz's fear.

Liz's first-choice candidate certainly fit that description: well qualified with impeccable credentials. In certain contexts, however, the "safe" choice becomes the riskiest one. That's often because we overestimate one risk and underestimate another. In this case, Liz thought that her lack of accounting experience represented the greatest risk. She optimized the search to solve that perceived weakness.

In fact, the greatest risk was that the candidate couldn't fit into the fast-moving start-up culture. Liz correctly assessed her relative financial skills but overprioritized the accounting functions given that the company was small and not that complicated. Despite knowing that "in smaller-company environments, one's ability to recognize patterns and think laterally is really critical," she didn't choose the candidate who had a "comfort level with a high degree of ambiguity or uncertainty."

She also underestimated her ability to help someone with less experience succeed. "I was sort of doubting that I don't think I know enough about this or am expert enough in this to coach someone and develop them. Well, that's bullshit; that's not true. I do it all the time with many different areas of our business that I oversee."

There's an old expression in business: "No one ever got fired for hiring IBM." Back when IBM represented the best of technology companies, the expression indicated that chief technology officers who wanted to avoid criticism should make the safe choice.

That kind of conservatism can leak into even young companies and get compounded by deep historical biases. In the office, not everyone has the same opportunity to take risks or make mistakes. Liz worked incredibly hard to secure her first CFO role. Just the title alone—chief financial officer—suggests the need for sobriety and caution.

Many people in new positions try to balance "fear" and "greed"— they want to neither miss out on the next idea nor look foolish by backing a dumb one. We all want the satisfaction of making a good decision yet fear taking too much risk. Anxiety plays a useful role in constraining stupidity, but avoiding risk completely feels like the path to an unsatisfying life.

It's hard to respect a librarian who worries so much about late returns that he doesn't lend any books. A loan officer who avoids losses by not lending any money has hardly succeeded.

From our childhood, we experience the benefits of risk-taking; research confirms that excessive error avoidance is counterproductive. Students benefit from making mistakes and getting corrected; teachers learn about their students through that process.[3] Allowing students to make mistakes in low-stakes environments improves their performance when the stakes get higher. The process increases knowledge while simultaneously reinforcing resiliency.

Extreme risk aversion may feel better in the moment but will likely lead to a different kind of mistake and regret. Psychologists describe some people as "prevention-" and others as "promotion-" focused.

Promotion-focused individuals focus on making good things happen, which leads them to have higher risk appetites that they use to pursue their goals.

Conversely, some prevention-focused people hate mistakes so much that they miss out on opportunities.[4] You won't fight with your partner if you never have one or give the wrong gift at Christmas if you don't go see your family.

Too much risk aversion creates different problems in the workplace. In a *Harvard Business Review* article, Greg McKeown, the author of *Effortless*, argues that leaders should encourage their employees to use the 85 percent rule: work to 85 percent capacity to prevent burnout, and strive for 85 percent right decisions to keep moving forward (rather than waiting for a 100 percent right decision).

McKeown cites research about two different types of perfectionists: "excellence-seeking" (people who hold high standards for themselves and others) and "failure-avoiding" (people who feel consistently anxious and worry that mistakes will cause them to lose the respect of their peers).[5] Excellence seekers often drive themselves and others crazy. Failure avoiders often don't take risks that would ultimately benefit themselves and their employers.

When perfectionists do make mistakes, they often engage in what Aaron Beck called all-or-nothing thinking.[6] That's when people think in extremes and judge themselves harshly for minor mistakes: "If I'm not perfect, I'm a disaster!" Ironically, the desire for perfection, coupled with an intensified allergy to mistakes, can stimulate mistakes, including avoiding opportunities where perfection is not guaranteed—most of life.

Liz recognized that feature of the situation—with one important overlay. "I think that had I been a White male, I probably would have felt freer to make mistakes." She felt that in so many of her early jobs. "It's really hard to sometimes carry the pressure of feeling 'If I fuck this up, I'm fucking it up for everybody.' Other people who look like me will have a harder time."

This echoes closely Karol Mason's experiences and what so many underrepresented minorities experience.

Now compound that feeling with the dynamics at Hello Sunshine, a small company where each individual had a greater impact, and which had attracted serious capital to one of the first female-led production companies. "I know that when we were starting Hello Sunshine, every single one of us on the executive team felt if we mess this up, if we don't do this right, they're going to say, like, 'Look, this is why women shouldn't be able to do X, Y, or Z.'"

It actually gets even harder, in certain respects, due to Liz's super-high performance.

"I found that there's this term we use a lot around 'overfunction-ing.'" Throughout her career, she had shouldered more than her share of work. At her investment bank, she carried two and a half times as many assignments as some of her colleagues. Her boss hadn't noticed until Liz mentioned it. Importantly, Liz hadn't said anything until it became so burdensome that she wanted to quit.

It all comes together: the burden that Black women face not to make mistakes, the desire in banking to appear superhuman (or to overfunc-tion), the pressure of having such a big CFO job so early in your career.

Those factors swirl around in a way that leads Liz to think that "it was a decision that was motivated by fear and self-doubt on my part . . . This was to be my security blanket. The person who is going to have all the answers."

When that person didn't have the answers because she couldn't work in that environment, did the company suffer? "The long-term impact of it? Minimal. It was a mistake I made. I fixed it. I identified it quickly. I brought in a candidate who is incredible, and so the scars [to the company] are minimal."

Why, when the company continued on so effectively, does she remember this mistake so clearly? Partly because she also knows that her decision led to another woman failing in her job.

Mostly because of how she felt at the time. "I guess that's the thing about the masks that we wear. Inside, there's this loop of 'God, you're a fucking idiot,' because I'm not giving myself permission to make mistakes."

As with so many people, her superpowers—working harder, performing better, demonstrating constant competence—come at a cost. "I can attribute a lot of my success to feeling like I had to be perfect. I had to be the most knowledgeable. . . . That's great. But then there's also a degree of exhaustion that comes with it."

She wonders about another cost. "It has done a disservice to me in terms of how free I've felt to make decisions." Among women of Liz's generation, you hear discussion of "effortless perfectionism"—the need to appear highly competent without appearing to expend significant effort—and the toll it can place on them. We interviewed Liz over Zoom right after she had moved and right before she was about to take a huge new job. Her background in the Zoom picture looked immaculate.

"You go into a situation and show up for work, and you don't show up as your full selves. It's kind of like how I have behind me now suitcases and piles of clothes that need to be unpacked. Would it be the end of the world if you saw them?"

Liz has come to recognize the cost of trying to appear perfect—both in her personal life and at work. Her hiring choice reflected an earlier tendency—based partly on her exceptional experiences—to avoid making risky decisions, which might undermine the perception of flawlessness. Now, having accomplished so much, she demonstrates more comfort with uncertainty.

15

Running Man

Interviewing Malcolm Gladwell made us anxious. Who wants to interview someone who interviews people for a living? If you host a cooking show, you probably wouldn't invite Ina Garten as your first guest.

We didn't know whether Malcolm had a mistake that he wanted to discuss, so we had a question prepared. When *Outliers* came out in 2008, it did not generate universal praise. One reviewer wrote, "The book, which purports to explain the real reason some people—like Bill Gates and the Beatles—are successful, is peppy, brightly written and provocative in a buzzy sort of way. It is also glib, poorly reasoned and thoroughly unconvincing."[1]

That wasn't the first time Malcolm had faced this kind of criticism. When *The Tipping Point* came out in 2000, this was one reaction: "His argument hinges on the seductive but questionable idea that certain extraordinary outcomes . . . can be explained by almost comically narrow factors."[2]

We asked Malcolm whether that criticism stung and whether those reviews and others like them reveal a pattern of mistakes beneath his hugely successful books. It turns out that Malcolm doesn't even read his reviews. He respects the careful academic research that reviewers generally prioritize. Yet while researchers rely on moderation, balance, and double-blind studies to fulfill their scholarly responsibilities, he has a different ambition.

He writes books to change the narrative on trends and widely held beliefs. To penetrate a saturated market, he writes with conviction and then markets his ideas with complete commitment. *The Tipping Point* sold over five million copies; *Outliers* millions more. That's his barometer of success. As a result, for our interview, he had a completely different mistake in mind.

If you think Malcolm competes hard as an author, you should have seen him as a teenager. In 1978, Malcolm, then a slight young man from Elmira, Ontario, set a new Canadian record in the boys-under-sixteen 1,500-meter race. He was only fourteen years old. The results book for the National Youth Track & Field Championships proclaims, "Future Olympians Start Here!" This young phenom looked headed in that direction. Instead, within less than two years, Malcolm quit running for decades. Not just racing. Running at all. "I engaged in an act of self-sabotage at fifteen and have regretted that decision through much of my adult life," Malcolm says. "One of the biggest mistakes that I've made."

As a child, Malcolm began running with his father and realized that he might have talent when his father couldn't keep up with him. Shortly thereafter, at age twelve, he joined the high school track team, where he started winning races despite being two years younger than his teammates. "Everyone was like, 'Oh, when you're at the top of your age class, you're going to do great,'" he remembers. "I got a lot of reinforcement. And I liked it. It was so much fun."

Malcolm loved running. "There's a feeling of running when it's coming easily. I remember when I was fourteen, I realized I couldn't tire myself out. When you're at that level of fitness, it's magic. I'll never forget those feelings of magic."

He also remembers just enjoying being so good at something. "I was as good a thirteen- and fourteen-year-old runner as there was out there. There was a guy called Dave Reid who was the dominant runner of my generation in Canada. When I was thirteen, I beat Dave Reid in this epic showdown. And then I beat him again when I was fourteen. And then Dave Reid went on to the Olympics."

Natural athleticism only gets you so far. Malcolm also had an uncanny attraction to the required discipline. "I have never stopped a workout before it was over. Never. If we're doing ten by four hundreds, we're doing ten by four hundreds. It'd be unthinkable. A lot of the pleasure comes from you setting a standard and you meeting a standard. That was very appealing to my kind of thirteen- and fourteen-year-old self. And that everything was timed. There was an order to it that was very appealing to me. Everyone runs the same course. Everyone is judged by the same standard. It was fair. There were no barriers. It was up to you how well you did."

Malcolm's view of running as the ultimate meritocracy served him well when he was winning. But then, after a couple years of being practically unbeatable, he started to lose—to boys his own age. "I won the National Championships one year, and then the next year I came in second and fourth. To this day, I think of those second- and fourth-place finishes as huge failures. I'd rarely been as disappointed in myself as I was then."

The losses stung so severely that Malcolm quit the track team. "I quit at fifteen and never raced competitively again.

"Why did I walk away from something like that?" The mistake fills him with regret.

When we make mistakes during an earlier stage of life, there's a natural temptation to superimpose our current beliefs and schemas on our younger selves. Malcolm does a good job of avoiding that trap. He puts himself back in the mind of a skinny teenage runner. "I would get nervous before big meets weeks in advance, tormented. There would be a long stretch before the race where I would convince myself I didn't want to run at all. There would always be a moment in the middle of the race where I would ask myself, 'Why am I doing this? What's the point?'"

"The psychological cost of dealing with all that nervousness and doubt . . . [was] so great that I couldn't continue doing it." Anxiety breeds avoidance. So, like many people who feel anxious, Malcolm opted out. As he puts it, "I was very successful in competition, but I hated to race. To this day, the only thing in my life that I've ever gotten nervous about is racing—nothing else makes me nervous."

He loved training; he loved winning; and then he became overwhelmed by the anxiety of potentially losing.

Just as we need to avoid imposing our adult schemas on our younger selves, it can help to consider how early mistakes shape our adult lives. The decision to quit reinforced two schemas that have heavily influenced Malcolm's professional and personal life. The first relates to money, the second to all-or-nothing thinking.

With the anxiety of running behind him, his days in a small high school in rural Canada were filled with friendship and freedom. "You know, intellectual pursuits or academic issues back then [had] a strong undercurrent of whimsy and mischief. I wasn't serious. My friend Terry and I treated high school like a kind of grand joke because we could do that.

"[We] wanted to subvert the system. We agreed that it was foolish to compete on grades. So we had to increase the degree of difficulty. We would multiply our averages by the number of absences we had.

We competed to see who could skip the most amount of school and still have the highest grades. That consumed the last two years of my high school."

Malcolm realized early that "writing all comes from some kind of tension between uncovering the rules and then uncovering the exceptions to the rules and delighting in the difference."

Against that backdrop of a carefree adolescence lay one source of family concern: money. Somehow even as a child Malcolm internalized his family's financial situation. "I remember as a kid I really, really, really, really wanted to subscribe to *Road & Track* magazine. I was probably eleven, and I saved all my money, and then I realized I didn't have enough, and I remember bursting into tears. I was like five dollars short [and my mother said], 'Why didn't you ask us?' I think I did not want to burden the family finances."

Malcolm had good reason to worry about the family's finances. "I realized, in retrospect, that [my father] was under a great deal of stress for money reasons. Canada in the 1970s . . . interest rates were in the twenties. Mortgage interest was not deductible, and he, my dad, built a house in 1978. And I realized that we got totally overextended. It must have been a very, very difficult period in his life."

Malcolm both understood the situation perfectly (his parents did feel financial pressure) and didn't have a clue (his parents could afford the small pleasures that he wanted as a child). He believes today that his financial concerns influenced his decision to quit running. Whether he knew it at the time or only realized it later, he associates running with financial instability. "What seems so exciting at sixteen is like a fucking disaster at twenty-eight, you know? The party's over. You can't make a career out of running."

Now, as an adult, he has a hard time fully untangling his anxiety about racing and his perceptions about his family's financial pressures.

"I spent years in therapy discussing this very question, which was that from a very early age it was clear to me that I had to take care of the family. That it was going to be down to me. And, in fact, that prophecy turned out to be one hundred percent true." Not all our schemas lead us down false paths.

It's possible to see his regret about quitting as partly a regret about the need to focus on financial independence at the expense of other pursuits.

Or, maybe, that very financial uncertainty coupled with the determination he learned as a runner helps explain his commitment to writing bestseller after bestseller. Malcolm clearly loves to write and takes pride in the ways his ideas have shaped popular culture, but he does not do it just for that reason. Book sales are a way of keeping score. Bestsellers not only demonstrate the popularity of what he writes; they have also provided remarkable financial security. Runners have their times; authors such as Malcolm have their sales.

Many runners focus on the personal bests—their fastest time at a given distance. They keep score against themselves. Malcolm saw the world differently. "I came to believe that the real enjoyment from running came from winning. And I won a lot, so it was very easy to conflate those two things. I think the reason I quit was I began to fear that I wouldn't win as reliably as I had been. I think that was my fear. I couldn't imagine enjoying it if I didn't win anymore."

That's partly because athletes can have mixed emotions even after the best wins or most painful losses. Personal records get set during losing efforts, and great stars can have mediocre performances in winning games. When a football team loses and a quarterback gloats about his personal stats or blames a receiver for dropping a crucial pass, he shouldn't expect much blocking in the next game.

In some cases, just getting to the game feels like a victory. Cinderella teams in the NCAA basketball tournament rarely look as devastated when they lose as higher-ranked ones. There's serious scholarship about why bronze-medal winners feel happier than their silver-medal competitors. Expectations heavily influence emotions. As in other aspects of life, just showing up can feel pretty good.

Josh once asked an offensive lineman why he loved playing football. He talked about the camaraderie and tactics, and the discipline and passion. Then he paused and said, "You know, if I could dig a ditch and have eighty thousand people cheer me on, I'd probably do that too."

In short, after a competition it's hard to know how athletes really feel or even why they want to compete at all. At first blush, winning seems like the key motivator, with the fear of losing playing a complementary role. That marries ideas that date back thousands of years. Epicurus wrote about the pursuit of pleasure and the corresponding avoidance of pain. Jeremy Bentham, the founder of utilitarianism, famously wrote, "Nature has placed mankind under the governance of two sovereign masters, pain and pleasure."[3]

Early psychologists recognized how these sensations drove behavior. In 1890, William James wrote that pleasure and pain were "springs of action"—pleasure a "tremendous reinforcer" and pain a "tremendous inhibitor."[4] In the 1930s and '40s, a new approach emerged, led by Kurt Lewin and Neal Miller. They recognized that many prospective actions do not imply either pleasure or pain: they often have both. Imagine that you've always wanted to eat Japanese food in Tokyo (pleasure) but worry about functioning in an environment where you don't know the language or mores (pain). Miller called this "approach-avoidance conflict" to capture the idea that we might want to simultaneously approach and avoid the same situation.[5]

In 2001, Andrew J. Elliot and Holly A. McGregor published a paper that provided a new way to consider the approach-avoidance conflict.[6] They built on an earlier realization that not everyone is motivated by a desire to win. Some people strive for mastery—the goal of perfecting a pursuit. The paper set out a 2 × 2 framework with performance (winning) and mastery on one side, and approach and avoidance on the other.

Unsurprisingly, approach goals, whether in pursuit of winning or mastery, led to higher performance and increased engagement. Subsequent studies have shown that framing tasks in terms of approach goals leads to greater satisfaction even when they produce the same results.

The framework helps us understand why some athletes can feel elated after achieving personal milestones in a "losing" effort. It also explains why some athletes become focused on avoiding situations where there's even a possibility of not winning. That's the thing about racing: there's no certainty about the outcome.

For Malcolm, running was about racing, and racing was about winning. It's the perspective of a perfectionist. He didn't want to race if he couldn't win, and he couldn't imagine running for any reason other than racing. Running became an all (winning) or nothing (losing) proposition. But even the best runners in the world win less than 50 percent of the time. So he chose nothing and quit.

He now sees how that schema of all-or-nothing thinking has led to a pattern of behavior throughout his life. "The fact that I would've stopped something that had such capacity for giving me pleasure has made me wonder about other life choices that I made. I had a very narrow definition of what joy was and what the path to happiness was. It's only now that I realize that is an unbelievably catastrophic conclusion to draw and that if you have that attitude in your life, you foreclose all manner of different choices."

Malcolm believes that all-or-nothing attitude got in the way of other major life decisions. Malcolm waited until relatively late in life to find a committed partner. Some might argue that for each of us only one person exists with whom we can find real happiness. Others believe that great relationships depend on flexibility and change, a belief that love overcomes the imperfections that we all have.

Well into his forties, Malcolm says, "I couldn't imagine settling down with someone and having a child unless I could have some guarantee that the person I settled down with was near perfect, the child is everything I wanted the child to be."

He sees an analogy to running, where "rather than risk an outcome that was less than perfect, I just walked away. With my personal relationships, it's sort of the same thing. Rather than risk an outcome that was less than perfect, I just declined to participate in the process at all."

He opted out—a binary decision that he regretted. Similarly, that kind of absolutism has cost him friendships and, at times, generated unproductive controversy. Part of the regret about running may relate to a deep realization that the binary approach has taken a toll on the rest of his life.

It's also worth remembering, however, that Malcolm's ability and willingness to take strong positions in opposition to conventional wisdom—the genesis of so many of his successful books—may relate to this kind of thinking. Writing a strongly argued book obviously differs from his regrettable teenage decision about running, but they both reflect an aspect of his personality that tends to paint bright lines through subtle situations. In his writing life, the ability to question the rules and take contrarian, strongly held views allows him to reimagine the way the world works. The capacity to think with such clarity and argue for his positions with such certainty has led to remarkable breakthroughs and success.

He attributes some of this skill—and some of the consequences—to his father, who encouraged vigorous debate and questioning of even the fundamental mathematical theories he taught. If you learn as a child that even math can have multiple answers, it may make you more willing to tune out the criticism of academic experts who question your conclusions.

It takes a special kind of talent and a willingness to take intellectual risk to write with Malcolm's confidence. If you're going to tell academics who've conducted thousands of hours of research that you have a different view, and if you want that idea to gain traction in the marketplace of ideas, you can't do it in half measures. And you have to accept the critical reviews that accuse you of oversimplification.

The regret that comes from an imagined but unrealized ambition, in this case becoming an Olympic runner, clearly feels painful. When seen in the context of the mindset that informed his decision to defer parenting or to endure the pain of ruptured friendships, the mistake takes on a power far greater than what we normally associate with an impetuous teenage decision.

Malcolm did finally return to running. And, no surprise, it happened after he found financial security. "When do I seriously return? In my early fifties. And, you know, that's when I found I was able to admit to myself that I had enough [financial security]."

He remembers the moment that he finally let go of his all-or-nothing attitude toward running. "I decided to go to the East River track one day. I was doing a workout on my own for fun. Then I noticed a group of people. And some of the people in the group who were running invited me to join them. They were a group of profoundly mediocre runners who my younger self would've disdained like, 'What am I doing with these people?'

"And I realized, these are people who run because they love running and they're never going to win. It was just so liberating. There was no status associated with it. I couldn't find the middle ground between racing and quitting, and now I think I have."

Almost as an afterthought, we asked about what made Malcolm such a great runner. We expected to hear about the combination of talent and hard work that defined so many characters in *Outliers*. We got a different answer. "God! Do I think you have an obligation to pursue the things that you're good at? I think the answer is yes, I think you do."

He brings an almost eighteenth-century Protestant approach to his pursuits: spend time on the gifts that God has granted you in abundance rather than the ones that make you happiest. Indeed, he uses the word "soft" to describe activities he does for enjoyment rather than accomplishment.

That's partly because he believes that "on a relative basis, I'm probably a better runner than I am at anything else. That's true." Maybe. Keep in mind that he wrote five books that made the *New York Times* bestseller list and that *Outliers* spent nearly five hundred weeks on it.

PART 3

Onward Through Openness

16

How to Talk About Mistakes

All our interviews and research, all the time spent unraveling our own mistakes, taught us so much about them and their consequences. It felt great. But it had also taken us four years! The duration of our effort reflected both our fears and our ignorance about how to do it. False starts led to dead ends; fresh starts prompted new frustrations. Slowly, through trial and error, we got better at interviewing each other and then the people with whom we spoke. We began to recognize patterns of behavior that informed our line of questioning.

Even from the start, we sensed that the more we talked and then wrote about our mistakes, the better we would feel. We knew that in all aspects of our lives, stories help us make sense of the world. The best narratives reveal cause and effect; they reveal the emotions and ideas that drive behavior. We just didn't know how to do it.

Now, after all our unsuccessful attempts, we have a road map—in the form of an acronym—for how to talk about your mistakes: disclose, unpack, empathize, and trust (DUET). This was, after all, a duet between two people trying to figure out what had happened. DUET is a process for sharing and normalizing mistakes so that we make fewer of them and so that they sting less. The acronym helped us encourage honesty; it reminded us to uncover hidden layers; it placed empathy at the center of our questioning; and it required trust. These steps destigmatized the unmentionable and surfaced its antecedents.

This is how you can try it out.

DISCLOSE

When we first tried to disclose our mistakes, it didn't go so well. We felt ashamed and uncomfortable. We didn't have any practice with the subject and couldn't see ourselves clearly. Bernard Baruch, the famous financier and presidential adviser, put it perfectly:

> I have known men who could see through the motivations of others with the skill of a clairvoyant; only to prove blind to their own mistakes. I have been one of those men.[1]

We couldn't hold a mirror up to ourselves. And when we did, embarrassment and pain distorted what we saw. Only through repeated discussion did we get comfortable enough to talk about the moments that had truly upset our lives. Repeatedly, we had to return to the scene of the crime.

Discussion takes practice, so the *D* in DUET does not stand for diving into the deep end. Start with a small mistake, avoid "shoulding" on yourself (e.g., I "should" have done this . . .),[2] and make it clear to whomever you speak that you do not want advice right away. There's nothing like unsolicited advice to make you want to stop sharing.

Daniel Kahneman and Gary Klein articulate the benefit of discussion, or what they called "educating gossip," which they thought would help you "talk about other people's mistakes in a more refined way."[3] That's a version of permission and encouragement to disclose what previously felt better hidden—including what you find buried beneath your mistake.

The "polar bear" that lies lurking in the recesses of your psyche suddenly becomes much less ferocious when it's revealed.

UNPACK

Once you start talking, remember the Russian nesting dolls: unpack what happened. There's no "best" way to unpack a mistake. Each one has different pathways and causes that require nimble questioning and patience. We learned through trial and error.

We also benefited from a methodology that psychologists call a behavioral analysis. When they want to figure out a behavior pattern, they examine and identify the ABCs.

A's are the antecedents of the behavior. B's are the target behavior they are trying to understand. And C's are the consequences of the behavior. They start by clearly identifying the B, which allows them to backtrack and figure out the A's—the antecedents—that precede and prompt the behavior. Then they move to the C's—the consequences—which are often rewards or punishments that increase or decrease, respectively, the likelihood of that behavior in the future.

For our work, we examined what happened during the mistake (the B's), before it (the A's), and after (the C's). The ABCs are another way of thinking about the three-act structure.

Below are some questions that align with this methodology. Most important, whether you're asking these questions of yourself or another person, emphasize empathy and curiosity, try to avoid judgment, and recognize that it will likely take at least several conversations to understand what happened and why.

If you want to start on your own, the research of Dr. James Penne-baker and his colleagues has demonstrated the benefit of writing down your thoughts.[4] Try constructing a narrative—the story of your mistake—that answers the questions below. You can start by writing out the answers directly or try telling the story the way that you would to a friend. It will help if you include cause and effect, or, as Penne-baker puts it, causality ("because") and self-awareness ("I realize").

Identify the mistake and the immediate context (the **during**):

1. *Definition:* As precisely as possible, what mistake did you actually make?
2. *Situation:* When and where did it happen? Who else was present, and how did they react?
3. *Context:* Did you know where you were and why?
4. *Self-awareness:* What was your mood at the time you made the mistake? What emotion did you feel while making it (e.g., anger, anxiety, embarrassment, jealousy, insecurity)?
5. *Recognition:* Did you know immediately that you had made a mistake?

Identify patterns and schemas (the **before**):

1. *Ex ante:* What happened in the hours and days before the mistake?
2. *Schemas:* Did you go into the situation with a preexisting set of assumptions (e.g., schemas) that didn't actually apply?
3. *Patterns:* Does this mistake remind you of other mis-takes you've made? Did they involve similar emotions, decision-making processes, or reaction times?

4. *Feedback:* What have friends and family told you about these types of mistakes?
5. *Processing:* Before this mistake, had you thought about any pattern of mistakes or the feedback that you had received?

Identify how you reacted (the **after**):

1. *Openness:* Have you told others about the mistake?
2. *Apologies:* Did you wrong others? Are there any apologies you feel that you should make? Do you need to repair any relationships because of the harm caused by your mistake?
3. *Forgiveness:* Have you forgiven yourself?
4. *Perspective:* Would you blame a friend for this mistake (e.g., are you being too hard on yourself)?
5. *Adaptation:* How did your understanding of yourself, how relationships work, or how the world works change because of this mistake? Did you change too little or too much?

As we described at the start of the book, many mistakes reflect deep societal flaws. When assessing your mistake, it may help to consider whether larger forces influenced your actions, or if the treatment you received reflected the conscious and unconscious biases that we all bring to interactions, and therefore whether you simply faced a situation where you had to choose between bad alternatives (similar to what Karol faced) or even seemingly good ones (what Liz felt).

Once you get the hang of it, then try to go deep. It's like weeding. If you just pull up the leaves of a dandelion, it will grow right back.

After each section, try to avoid a "eureka" moment. Be especially careful about jumping to conclusions about causality. For example, you may recall crying, which we usually associate with sadness. Yet, we all cry for so many different reasons: physical pain, embarrassment, joy. By asking "Why was I crying?" you can unpack the underlying cause more effectively.

Try to regain how you felt as a child, in your best learning environments, when mistakes served as an essential part of learning. Long before we knew about the Five Whys, our best teachers consistently encouraged curiosity and flexibility. Now when we make mistakes, we try to practice the expression "curious, not furious." Instead of getting mad at ourselves or others, we're trying to find fascination in what happened and why.

EMPATHIZE

No matter how excited you become, confused by what you find, or incredulous about the answers, try to ask questions gently. Donald Winnicott, the British pediatrician and psychoanalyst, wrote extensively about "holding environments"—the psychological space a parent or caregiver gives a child so that the child feels safe and supported. That holding environment allows children to learn from their mistakes instead of hiding them. Even as adults, we can try to create a similar environment for these kinds of conversations.

So that's the *E* in DUET: empathize. When we unpacked our mistakes, we didn't always like what we found. The root causes, our underlying schemas and insecurities, sometimes felt even uglier than the mistakes themselves. That's why it's so important to remember the advice of psychologist Albert Ellis, the father of "unconditional self-acceptance." Ellis believed that we all have irrational beliefs about our capacity for perfection. By practicing unconditional self-acceptance, we can acknowledge our flaws and mistakes, accept them as part of our humanity, and reassure ourselves that our imperfections do not make us unworthy of love.[5]

Acceptance allows us to stop hiding our mistakes; empathy creates the space for honesty. Honesty encourages the psychological flexibility that allows us to adjust our schemas constructively through assimilation and accommodation: adding information to preexisting schemas, altering old ones, or creating new ones.[6] If you demonstrate empathy to yourself and the people with whom you're talking, it will encourage the kind of disclosure that can lead to beneficial change.

TRUST

All these discussions require one final element: trust—in yourself and others. The first time we revealed our mistakes it felt deeply uncomfortable, but we trusted each other not to pass judgment. It proved harder to trust ourselves. The disclosure leap requires you to trust the person who's listening and asking questions—especially if it's just yourself.

Here's one technique that can help. Imagine the worst possible outcome: that everyone learns about your mistake and what caused it. The Stoics called it *premeditatio malorum* (premeditation of evils), and they used it to lessen the emotional impact of potentially painful events. When we told friends about this book, some reacted with horror: "Why would you want people to know about your stupidity?"

We envisioned the ridicule we might endure and had to trust that our family and friends would not think the worst of us. The people with whom you're closest will know that your mistakes do not define you. Indeed, we believe that if you trust them with your honesty, it will deepen your friendships just as it did ours.

As you talk to your friends and family, you may hit an emotional roadblock. Try to sit with the discomfort and untangle its roots. At other moments it will come flowingly. Enjoy it. Then, try to avoid dashing through it. We constantly felt humbled by how little we understood and how many layers we still needed to explore.

At times we blew it. And you will too. The history got too heavy and our questions neither illuminated the underlying issues nor demonstrated empathy. We didn't just drop the ball; we broke something more fragile. That moment, when it felt like our work together had damaged our friendship, led to the image on the cover of this book.

Art historians believe that in the fifteenth century, the shogun Ashikaga Yoshimasa sent a broken bowl back to China for repairs. It came back with unattractive staples holding it together. In their search for a better solution, Japanese artisans created *kintsugi*, which uses gold to fill cracks in precious objects.

Followers of *kintsugi* believe that the repaired item becomes even more beautiful, as it embodies *wabi-sabi* (imperfections represent the natural cycle of growth and decay) as well as *mushin* (the practice of acceptance).

We now believe that while mistakes cause cracks in our relationships and work, our exploration of them helps heal those fissures in ways that enrich and strengthen our lives. Recognizing our imperfections led to acceptance. Of course, that didn't stop us from thinking about how to just avoid making mistakes in the first place.

17

How to Make Fewer Mistakes

D UET provides a guide for how to talk about your mistakes. But what about just making fewer of them? That's Charlie Munger's advice (Munger was Warren Buffett's partner at Berkshire Hathaway): "I've made my way in life by making fewer mistakes than others. I've just avoided them. If you try to be consistently not stupid, instead of trying to be very intelligent, you'll end up being wise and make fewer mistakes."[1]

Easier said than done. If we had a simple answer to Munger's advice, we would have written a shorter book. Instead, we believe that unpacking mistakes, learning about our schemas, and forgiving ourselves leads to greater happiness and, yes, making fewer mistakes. The stories you've read represent the lived experience of mistakes. We also know this approach takes time and patience.

So, here are three "shortcuts" that can help you make fewer mistakes. First, take a deep breath. Second, remember to balance between making decisions instinctively (including by relying on our schemas) and acting more deliberately. And third, sometimes focus on what not to do.

First, taking a deep breath or a "cheetah pause" prevents us from rushing into a bad decision. It's a way of self-regulating our reactions. It's helpful to remember Groucho Marx's line: "Speak when you are angry and you will make the best speech you will ever regret."[2]

That pause also allows us to avoid the risk of compounding our mistakes. When in doubt, remember what befell the children in *The Cat in the Hat*: one poor decision leads to another and chaos ensues. It's bad enough to let the Cat into your life, but you certainly don't need Thing 1 and Thing 2 making everything even worse.

Whether you're angry or sympathetic, depressed or euphoric, try to find the time and space to step back from the situation before you speak or act. If possible, take the pot off the stove; let your emotions stop boiling before you act. That will allow you to apply all your experience, judgment, and intellect before you act.

The more important the mistake, the deeper it goes, the more important it becomes to slow down. Willie Mosconi, the most famous billiards player of the twentieth century, once described the difference between a professional and an amateur pool player. When amateurs hit a streak, they go around the table at an ever-increasing speed. They're caught up in the euphoria of their success. Eventually, of course, something goes wrong.

Great professionals such as Mosconi never lose their composure. They proceed around the table with the same measured pace regardless of whether they are making great shots or not. As you unpack your mistakes, remember Mosconi. Give yourself the time and composure to study the questions and the answers.

The second shortcut: remember that you will make the best decisions if you use all your mental faculties. Here it's helpful to remember *Star Trek*—the series, the movies, and the spin-offs. One recurring element embodied the varied ways we make decisions: the running battle between Captain Kirk ("Intuition, however illogical, . . . is recognized as a command prerogative") and Spock ("That is illogical, Captain").[3]

The argument feels, well, intuitive. How often has someone told you to "trust your gut" or "do the math"? Both make sense and have value. Yet, good decisions often require us to tap our intellects and our emotions. Some investors overthink situations, which prevents them from making decisions. Others just go with their gut—that's really just a form of gambling. The best investors balance the two.

Mistakes often occur when we rely too heavily on one or the other instead of balancing both. When our emotions take over and run amok, and mistakes arise, you often hear people ask, "What were you thinking?" The answer, of course, is that you weren't "thinking" at all.

Or sometimes, we think too much. In *Descartes' Error: Emotion, Reason, and the Human Brain*, neuroscientist Antonio Damasio argues that we depend on emotions to make good decisions.[4] Using research on patients with brain injuries that affect their emotional processes, he shows that they struggle to make wise choices even if they have not lost their ability to reason. Neither intellect nor emotions in isolation serve us well.

As humans, we're constantly balancing our shortcuts, emotions, and intellects to find the right answer. Our biology (genetics), family history (religion, culture, and interpersonal dynamics), and our lived experiences shape how we process the information that floods our senses. Just when we think we have it figured out, we feel anxious about what we've decided, so we reverse ourselves or our emotions make us jump to the wrong conclusion.

For the first half of the twentieth century, people thought that either our emotions and the subconscious (think of them as the Freudians) or our intellects (think of them as rationalists) drive us. To oversimplify, psychiatrists worked on our emotional responses; economists conducted experiments that demonstrated our capacity for rational responses.

In the 1960s and '70s, a new field emerged that radically altered our thinking: behavioral economics. Led by psychology professors Daniel Kahneman and Amos Tversky, this field suggested that individuals didn't always act in ways that traditional economics would consider rational. They combined psychology, neuroscience, and economics to construct frameworks for how people make decisions.

Academics and students of human nature followed their work from almost their initial publications; the public became much more aware of it following the release of *Thinking, Fast and Slow* in 2011.[5] That book highlighted the difference between System 1 (nearly spontaneous thought based on instinct, emotion, and experience) and System 2 (reasoned, conscious consideration).

When we process information automatically using System 1, we tend to fit the data into gross categories, following rough schemas and heuristics, and while it can serve us well, it can also lead to more mistakes. In contrast, our secondary/reflective processing system (System 2) processes information more rationally and slowly, and requires more conscious effort on our part. These two systems can work together. For example, beliefs generated by the automatic system can be assessed and corrected by the reflective system.

Jonathan Haidt, in *The Happiness Hypothesis: Finding Modern Truth in Ancient Wisdom*,[6] has a nice metaphor for a version of System 1 and System 2 processes: "The mind is divided, like a rider on an elephant, and the rider's job is to serve the elephant."[7] For Haidt, the elephant represents our instincts and morals (System 1); our minds (System 2) can help drive the elephant, but at times elephants are simply uncontrollable.

All the way back to Socrates and Plato, philosophers have advocated for the dialectic: the importance of keeping conflicting thoughts in your mind as a way of validating our ideas and illuminating the truth. We usually think about the dialectic in those terms: one idea is better than the other. The weaker idea serves as a foil to highlight the stronger.

Importantly, that's not always the case. Two contradictory ideas can both be true and separated by the word "and." We lead much of our lives making trade-offs between truths rather than just following the one true path. It's especially complicated because our truths can involve both rational ideas and powerful emotions. Sometimes, especially in politics, two rational ideas come into conflict: "I hate all the money in politics, and I feel the need to support candidates I admire" or "I love how immigrants have helped the United States, and I think we should have secure borders."

In other cases, two emotions contradict each other: "Graduating from college makes me happy, and I'm sad about no longer living with all my friends" or "I love my family, and sometimes they really annoy me."

Finally, deeply felt emotions and hard logic often battle it out: "I love spending time with this friend, and I know he encourages my bad habits" or "I hate needles, and I know that I need to get a flu shot." Internal conflicts often lead to the kind of confusion that undermines good decisions.

Those occasions when our feelings and intellects collide often lead to the greatest distress. Giving our emotions primacy makes us feel illogical. Relying too heavily on our intellects can take the joy and humanity out of life. The more stressful the situation, the harder it becomes to summon the perspective to decide which "truth" should matter most.

In the 1980s, psychology picked up on the ancient philosophers when the American psychologist Marsha Linehan developed dialectical behavior therapy (DBT). Linehan combined mindfulness from the Buddhist tradition with CBT to help patients with mental health disorders regulate their emotions through a combination of acceptance and change.

Linehan's acknowledgment of the difficulty of balancing emotion and logic led her to encourage the use of a Wise Mind: "Wise Mind is the integration of opposites: emotion mind and reasonable mind. You cannot overcome emotion mind with reasonable mind. Nor can you create emotions with reasonableness. You must go within and bring the two together."[8]

The Wise Mind captures a state where we decide based on the overlap between emotional and rational reactions. Linehan describes that deeply grounded feeling—even in highly stressful situations—when we're able to summon both sides in order to reach a decision that feels intuitively and logically correct.

Imagine that in confidence you tell your boss a piece of personal information that he then proceeds to share in a group meeting. Your Emotion Mind might want you to quit on the spot given your anger about the extreme violation of your trust. Your Reasonable Mind might quickly remind you of your upcoming mortgage payments. Your Wise Mind might schedule a meeting to tell your boss in private that he should have respected your privacy. By setting a boundary, you address your understandable anger (Emotion Mind) and don't kill your credit score by losing your job (Reasonable Mind).

The first two techniques for avoiding mistakes—taking a pause and using the full range of your faculties—help us control the elephant. If you look at jockeys at the Kentucky Derby or F1 racers in Monaco, they all look remarkably calm even though one small error could have a fatal impact. That works well for professionals, but those affirmative goals can get compromised in stressful situations.

So, here's the third part of how to avoid mistakes: try to avoid certain behaviors. Sometimes it's easier to remember what not to do.

You can find lots of useful advice about avoiding blunders from writers such as Adam Robinson, Shane Parrish, Anne-Laure Le Cunff, and Cheryl Strauss Einhorn. When you list all of their insights, you also get back to our "seven deadly sins" problem: there are just so many things to avoid.

Rather than include each of them, we've picked a few of our favorites that don't repeat the ones we've already described (e.g., avoid peer pressure, don't succumb to perfectionism):

1. *Avoid the expression "What the hell."*[9] When on a diet, many of us might still dig into a pint of ice cream after a tough day at work. We might even say "What the hell" as we open the freezer door.

2. *Watch out for information incoherence:* Too much information, too little, and the wrong type make it incredibly hard to analyze anything effectively.

3. *Don't act alone:* Study after study shows that diverse groups of individuals make better decisions. For the purpose of avoiding mistakes, consulting just one person counts as a group! Friends and colleagues can act as guardrails by keeping your behavior from straying into the land of mistakes.

4. *Don't succumb to fear of a better option (FOBO):* The insidious twin of FOMO can prove paralyzing. The fear or hope that a more optimal opportunity will come along can defer decision-making for as long as possible.[10] Put differently, avoid "analysis paralysis" and then do not dwell on your other "possible selves."

5. *Don't go to sleep feeling angry at yourself or others:* There are few mistakes that a serious apology can't help

cure. The sooner it comes, and the greater the sincerity with which it is delivered, the more it helps. Conversely, accepting an apology and allowing your anger to dissipate is the first step in reducing the risk that the problem compounds. In *The Power of Apology: Healing Steps to Transform All Your Relationships* by Beverly Engel, she describes the elements of a genuine apology, including assuming responsibility, expressing remorse, and committing to change.[11] Advice that's well worth following.

One final pattern to avoid: overuse of mental shortcuts. Yes, they can help us act quickly and decisively; they can also drive meaningful mistakes. Earlier in the book we described examples of how heuristics such as representativeness can make us overly reliant on mental prototypes. Here's one final example: recognition.

Gerd Gigerenzer, in *Gut Feelings: The Intelligence of the Unconscious*, describes an experiment in which researchers asked a group of American college students if Detroit or Milwaukee has a larger population. The students split their answers almost evenly. The researchers then asked a group of German students the same question. The Germans virtually all chose Detroit—the correct answer.[12]

Gigerenzer uses the story to illustrate how sometimes too much knowledge and thought can lead to poor decisions. The American students knew a lot about both cities, including their histories and locations. The Germans had simply heard of Detroit—and not Milwaukee—so they assumed Detroit had the larger population. The German students associated "well-known" with "large" based on their knowledge of other major foreign cities. In this case, the heuristic worked.

Now ask yourself whether Columbus, Ohio, or Las Vegas, Nevada, has a larger population. The latter has greater mindshare; the former is almost one third larger. That's the risk with mental shortcuts.

Then, when you've tried all these techniques for avoiding mistakes, and after you've still made a mistake you regret, just keep in mind what Richard Wollheim wrote, in a book about the philosopher F. H. Bradley: "On those who are so confident where the emotions end and the intellect begins, it is the pleasure and the privilege of the emotions to take their revenge."[13]

Ugly emotions. The very thing we had tried to bury for all the years before we began to talk about our mistakes. They grew and grew in darkness and shame and then reminded us of a movie that terrified us as teenagers.

18

The Water Is Lovely

The opening minutes of Ridley Scott's 1979 movie, *Alien*, resemble so many science fiction stories that preceded it. The movie stars Sigourney Weaver as the badass warrant officer on the *Nostromo*, a spaceship that responds to a distress signal from another ship. When she and her squad go to investigate, an alien attaches itself to a crew member's face. So far, so bad, another movie where aliens attack humans. Back aboard the *Nostromo*, the crew member, played by John Hurt, appears to recover. Then, unexpectedly, with intense savagery, an alien erupts from Hurt's chest.

Sitting in theaters thousands of miles apart, we can both remember the shock and terror of watching Hurt explode. We grew up watching aliens attack planet Earth, and monsters such as Godzilla emerge from the center of Earth. Never before, with anything like the gore and violence in *Alien*, had we witnessed the danger bursting out of a man who minutes earlier had appeared healthy.

Why does that movie, all these years later, stay so firmly lodged in our minds?

Horror movies can fall into two broad genres: the danger "within," and the danger "without." Sure, the danger without can scare us: psychotic escapees axe through doors, zombies rise from the dead. Message received: stay somewhere safe, avoid the stranger, beware of what lurks outside of view. At least when the danger comes from without, you can hide or kill it.

That's what heroes do. They kill monsters and villains. What happens, however, when the danger lurks within? That's the alien bursting out of John Hurt's chest, the devil that inhabits Linda Blair's body in *The Exorcist*. These movies terrify us because the danger is in us; we fear, like cancer, the damage caused by what grows within us. No hero can save us from ourselves. And no one looks heroic by confronting themselves.

When we started to think about our mistakes, we thought the danger came from without: the North Koreans who hacked Sony, the congressional investigators who put Josh's diary on the front pages. In writing this book, however, we came to realize that those events didn't happen to us. Mistakes weren't made. We made them. Passive verbs don't apply to what we did.

Then we let the aftermath become a danger within: a malevolent force that we could not control. We used suppression, avoidance, and change of direction to avoid confronting the root cause of the mistake. By refusing to understand our schemas, we allowed them to mutate, and we lost our ability to identify why we made our mistakes.

We really had two problems: we didn't know what had driven our mistakes, and we didn't want to let out what little we knew and felt. Why had we not realized earlier that discovery and then disclosure would reduce our reticence? When we were growing up, almost every aspect of our educational and social lives focused on men who had confronted the danger without. We were taught to focus on those attributes that drive success—bravery, focus, selflessness—and suppress those emotions that thwarted advancement—fear, ambivalence, compassion.

When the danger lurks within, it requires a new discovery process. For years, when we made mistakes, we quickly said things like "I wasn't myself" or "I wasn't thinking clearly." We now believe that in many cases our mistakes actually represent exactly who we are. Not us at our best, or how we are all the time, but who we are when our schemas exert undue influence or when we don't give ourselves time to process our environments. And who we are when we don't effectively process what happens after we make a mistake. Our mistakes are a bit like the bacteria in our stomachs: unique to each of us, essential to our healthy development, and not nearly as unseemly as we once thought.

We needed to follow the example of all those people who knew that shame dies when you let it out of its cage. We needed to talk our mistakes to death. That seems obvious now. Now that we know about the polar bear and our schemas. Now that we know that our rational minds only carry us so far.

Revealing what felt like a shameful secret made us feel lighter and stronger. The secret lost its potency as soon as we understood it better.

We knew none of this when we first walked along the beach talking about mistakes. On that cold fall day, as the wind whipped the sand into our eyes and grabbed the foam off the tops of the waves, our mistakes looked as gray and daunting as the Atlantic. Discussing them seemed as inviting as taking a swim.

But the seasons changed, our toes got used to the water, and we acclimated. What had seemed so scary and foreboding, what had looked so cold and uninviting, now gives us buoyancy. We laugh a little harder when the occasional wave sends us tumbling. We feel grateful for the sting of the salt water and the tug of the current.

We turn to our friends and families, and all of you, and call out, "Come on in. The water is lovely."

Acknowledgments

People of astonishing talent helped us with this book. When you read their names, you might wonder how they allowed what we wrote to appear in print. Do not blame them. We alone are responsible.

From the outset, we knew we needed expert advice and had the great good fortune to meet Professor Alison Papadakis. Alison has a deep and varied understanding of the relevant psychological literature coupled with an empathetic soul. Even beyond her academic expertise, she lived with us in the storytelling. She generated the trust that allowed us to tell her about our mistakes and respect her opinions about their roots. We simply could not have written about ourselves or others without her help. Our thanks do not do justice to the extent of her contribution.

Early in our process, Malcolm Gladwell, Michael Lewis, and Jacob Weisberg gave us very helpful structural suggestions. Michael May, who's an elegant editor, entered the process in the late innings, gave us insightful comments, and then stepped back into the shadows so that we could maintain our voice. At the very end of the process, when it was too late to take all of his good advice, David Shipley offered perceptive edits. All of their reputations should remain unsullied by what we have written.

Acknowledgments

We felt so fortunate to find an extraordinary group of research assistants and advisors. Dinda Elliott gave us wise, patient counsel long before we even had an outline. Stacey Kalish brought a lovely storyteller's sensibility to the project. Christina Ferguson's curiosity and resourcefulness helped us find compelling mistakes and useful insights. Megan Abate patiently and carefully untangled our interviews. Moses Tannenbaum applied his prodigious intellect against tasks that only utilized a small portion of his abilities. Simon Lieber reviewed the manuscript with incredible diligence. Elizabeth Hazelton and Allison McLean thoughtfully amplified our message. Alisa Isenberg kept us organized with her stunning calm and good humor. We thank them all.

All the people whose mistakes we described in this book, and those whose stories escaped these pages, risked making an even bigger one when they agreed to participate. They believed in us long before any evidence existed to support their decision. They then showed us remarkable grace as we tried to interpret their stories. They all have our deep and abiding gratitude.

Writers could look far and wide without finding a better agent than Kim Witherspoon. Her credibility put us on the path to publication; her experience made hard decisions look easy; and her sangfroid kept us focused and motivated when our enthusiasm faltered. We deeply thank Kim and her team of Jessica Mileo, Naomi Eisenbeiss, and Alexis Hurley.

Shannon Welch, our editor, had the unenviable task of helping us turn our proposal into a book. Leaving aside the generous risk that she took by deciding to work with us at all, she then had to help us shape and reshape a book that did not follow traditional norms. She navigated the process with aplomb by allowing us to run with our vision while firmly and thoughtfully pushing us to improve our structure and writing. She picked her spots carefully, made her case convincingly, and then let us reach our own conclusions. We have deep gratitude and respect for her and her team of Megan Noes, Jofie Ferrari-Adler, Alison Forner, Allison Green, Sara Kitchen, Ilana Gold, and Meredith Vilarello.

For years, our wives and children listened graciously as we droned on about our mistakes. They have always known that they have our unending love. Now they know that they also have our formal gratitude.

Notes

1: IT'S TIME

1. Erik H. Erikson, *Childhood and Society*, 2nd ed. (New York: W. W. Norton, 1963), 268.
2. Aristotle, *The "Art" of Rhetoric*, trans. John Henry Freese (Cambridge, MA: Harvard University Press, 1926), 109.
3. Sarah Shaw, *The Spirit of Buddhist Meditation* (New Haven, CT: Yale University Press, 2014), 58.
4. R. J. Zwi Werblowsky and Geoffrey Wigoder, eds., *The Oxford Dictionary of the Jewish Religion*, 1st ed. (New York: Oxford University Press, 1997), under "Sin," 646.
5. Kathryn Schulz, *Being Wrong: Adventures in the Margin of Error* (New York: HarperCollins, 2010), 5.
6. James Reason, *Human Error* (Cambridge, UK: Cambridge University Press, 1990), 9.
7. Barry A. J. and David R. Fisher, *Techniques of Crime Scene Investigation*, 9th ed. (Boca Raton, FL: CRC Press, 2022).
8. George Saunders, *A Swim in the Pond in the Rain* (New York: Random House, 2021), 227.
9. Syd Field, *Screenplay: The Foundations of Screenwriting* (New York: Dell Publishing, 1979).

Notes

2: KNOW THY SCHEMA

1. W. F. Brewer and J. C. Treyens, "Role of Schemata in Memory for Places," *Cognitive Psychology* 13, no. 2 (April 1981): 207–30.
2. Henry David Thoreau, *The Writings of Henry David Thoreau: Journal*, ed. Bradford Torrey (Boston: Houghton Mifflin, 1906), 2:373.
3. Aaron T. Beck, *Depression: Causes and Treatment* (Philadelphia: University of Pennsylvania Press, 1970), 282.
4. Jean Piaget, *The Language and Thought of the Child* (New York: Harcourt, 1926).
5. A. T. Beck and D. J. Dozois, "Cognitive Therapy: Current Status and Future Directions," *Annual Review of Medicine* 62 (2011): 397–409.
6. David Foster Wallace, *This Is Water* (New York: Little, Brown, 2009), 3–4.
7. Beck and Dozois, "Cognitive Therapy," 397–409.
8. C. G. Jung, *Aion: Researches into the Phenomenology of the Self*, trans. R. F. C. Hull (Princeton, NJ: Princeton University Press, 1969), 71.
9. Daniel M. Wegner, *White Bears and Other Unwanted Thoughts* (New York: Viking, 1989).
10. D. Cioffi and J. Holloway, "Delayed Costs of Suppressed Pain," *Journal of Personality and Social Psychology* 64, no. 2 (February 1993): 274–82.
11. Daniel M. Wegner, "You Can't Always Think What You Want: Problems in the Suppression of Unwanted Thoughts," *Advances in Experimental Social Psychology* 25 (1992): 220.

3: THE VELVET ROPE

1. *American Psychiatric Association, Diagnostic and Statistical Manual of Mental Disorders*, 5th ed. (Arlington, VA: American Psychiatric Association, 2013), 271.
2. Patricia A. Resick and Monica K. Schnicke, *Cognitive Processing Therapy for Rape Victims: A Treatment Manual*, 2nd ed. (Newbury Park, CA: Sage Publications, 1996).
3. Solomon E. Asch, "Effects of Group Pressure Upon the Modification

and Distortion of Judgments," in *Groups, Leadership and Men: Research in Human Relations*, ed. Harold Guetzkow (Pittsburgh: Carnegie Press, 1951), 177–90.

4. G. S. Berns et al., "Neurobiological Correlates of Social Conformity and Independence During Mental Rotation," *Biological Psychiatry* 58, no. 3 (August 2005): 245–53.

5. M. J. Salganik, P. S. Dodds, and D. J. Watts, "An Experimental Study of Inequality and Unpredictability in an Artificial Cultural Market," *Science* 311, no. 5762 (February 10, 2006): 854–56, https://www.science.org/doi/10.1126/science.1121066.

6. Naomi I. Eisenberger, Matthew D. Lieberman, and Kipling D. Williams, "Does Rejection Hurt? An fMRI Study of Social Exclusion," *Science* 302, no. 5643 (October 2003): 290–92, https://doi.org/10.1126/science.1089134.

4: THE POLAR BEAR

1. Seneca, *Ad Lucilium Epistulae Morales*, trans. Richard M. Gummere (London: William Heinemann, 1917), 1:75.

2. William Godwin, *Mandeville: A Tale of the Seventeenth Century in England* (Edinburgh: Archibald Constable and Co., 1817), 3:48.

3. Coralie Bastin et al., "Feelings of Shame, Embarrassment and Guilt and Their Neural Correlates: A Systematic Review," *Neuroscience & Biobehavioral Reviews* 71 (December 2016): 455–71.

4. Jessamyn West, *To See the Dream* (New York: Harcourt, Brace and Company, 1957), 181.

5. West, *To See the Dream*.

6. Bastin et al., "Feelings of Shame, Embarrassment and Guilt."

7. Henry David Thoreau, *The Writings of Henry David Thoreau: Journal*, ed. Bradford Torrey (Boston: Houghton Mifflin, 1906), 1:95.

8. Alice Boyes, "How to Stop Obsessing Over Your Mistakes," *Harvard Business Review*, February 25, 2019, https://hbr.org/2019/02/how-to-stop-obsessing-over-your-mistakes/.

9. Ethan Kross, *Chatter: The Voice in Our Head, Why It Matters, and How to Harness It* (New York: Crown, 2021).

10. Daniel M. Wegner, "You Can't Always Think What You Want: Problems in the Suppression of Unwanted Thoughts," *Advances in Experimental Social Psychology* 25 (1992): 195.

5: THE LIFE CYCLE OF MISTAKES

1. Danny Meyer, *Setting the Table: The Transforming Power of Hospitality in Business* (New York: HarperCollins, 2006), 223.

7: THE LUNCH BOX

1. Sigmund Freud, *Dream Psychology* (New York: James A. McCann, 1921), x.
2. Nancy D. Chase, ed., *Burdened Children: Theory, Research, and Treatment of Parentification* (Thousand Oaks, CA: Sage, 1999).

8: *THE BIG YEAR*

1. Angelique Chrisafis, "Brangelina Babies Arrive—Now for the Photoshoot," *The Guardian*, July 14, 2008, https://www.theguardian.com/lifeandstyle/2008/jul/14/celebrity.usa.
2. Mark R. Leary, Ellen S. Tambor, Sonja K. Terdal, and Deborah L. Downs, "Self-Esteem as an Interpersonal Monitor: The Sociometer Hypothesis," *Journal of Personality and Social Psychology* 68, no. 3 (January 1995): 518–30.
3. Nikhila Mahadevan, Aiden P. Gregg, and Constantine Sedikides, "Is Self-Regard a Sociometer or a Hierometer? Self-Esteem Tracks Status and Inclusion, Narcissism Tracks Status," *Journal of Personality and Social Psychology* 116, no. 3 (March 2019): 444–66.
4. Allan Fenigstein et al., "Public and Private Self-Consciousness: Assessment and Theory," *Journal of Consulting and Clinical Psychology* 43, no.4 (August 1975): 522–27.
5. Georg Simmel, *The Sociology of Georg Simmel*, ed., trans., Kurt H. Wolff (New York: Free Press, 1950), 403.
6. Kenneth A. Dodge, David C. Schlundt, Iris Schocken, and Judy

Notes# Notes

D. Delugach, "Social Competence and Children's Sociometric Status: The Role of Peer Group Entry Strategies," *Merrill-Palmer Quarterly* 29, no. 3 (1983): 309–36.

9: TRAFFIC STOP

1. Claude Steele and Joshua Aronson, "Stereotype Threat and the Intellectual Test Performance of African Americans," *Journal of Personality and Social Psychology* 69, no. 5 (1995): 797–811.
2. Laura J. Kray, Leigh Thompson, and Adam Galinsky, "Battle of the Sexes: Gender Stereotype Confirmation and Reactance in Negotiations," *Journal of Personality and Social Psychology* 80, no. 6 (2001): 942–58.
3. Caryn J. Block et al., "Contending with Stereotype Threat at Work: A Model of Long-Term Responses," *Counseling Psychologist* 39, no. 4 (May 2011): 570–600.
4. R. G. Tedeschi and L. G. Calhoun, "Posttraumatic Growth: Conceptual Foundations and Empirical Evidence," *Psychological Inquiry* 15, no. 1 (2004): 1–18.

10: THREE'S COMPANY

1. Announcement, *Cosmopolitan*, vol. 1 (March 1886), Scribd, https://www.scribd.com/document/621099404/Cosmopolitan-Volume-1-1886.
2. Anne-Marie Slaughter, "Why Women Still Can't Have It All," *The Atlantic*, July/August 2012, https://www.theatlantic.com/magazine/archive/2012/07/why-women-still-cant-have-it-all/309020/.
3. Peter Salovey and John D. Mayer, "Emotional Intelligence," *Imagination, Cognition and Personality* 9, no. 3 (March 1990): 185–211.

11: TO *ELLE* AND BACK

1. "The OODA Loop: How Fighter Pilots Make Fast and Accurate Decisions," *Farnam Street*, https://fs.blog/ooda-loop/.

2. Kristina L. Guo, "DECIDE: A Decision-Making Model for More Effective Decision Making by Health Care Managers," *Health Care Manager* 27, no. 2 (April 2008): 118–27.

3. Jerald H. Moxley, K. Anders Ericsson, Neil Charness, and Ralf T. Krampe, "The Role of Intuition and Deliberative Thinking in Experts' Superior Tactical Decision-Making," *Cognition* 124, no. 1 (July 2012): 72.

4. Cheryl Strauss Einhorn, "11 Myths and Decision-Making," *Harvard Business Review*, April 20, 2021, https://hbr.org/2021/04/11-myths-about-decision-making.

5. Stephen R. Covey, Foreword in *Prisoners of Our Thoughts: Viktor Frankl's Principles at Work* by Alex Pattakos (San Francisco: Berrett-Kohler Publishers, 2004), viii.

12: IT'S NOT HAVING WHAT YOU WANT; IT'S WANTING WHAT YOU HAVE

1. Gordon G. Gallup Jr., "Chimpanzees: Self-Recognition," *Science* 167, no. 3914 (January 1970), https://www.science.org/doi/10.1126/science.167.3914.86/.

13: PORTRAIT OF AN ARTIST AS A YOUNG MAN

1. Hazel Markus and Paula Nurius, "Possible Selves," *American Psychologist* 41, no. 9 (1986): 954–69.

2. Thomas Gilovich and Victoria Husted Medvec, "The Experience of Regret: What, When, and Why," *Psychological Review* 102, no. 2 (1995): 379–95.

3. Shai Davidai and Thomas Gilovich, "The Ideal Road Not Taken: The Self-Discrepancies Involved in People's Most Enduring Regrets," *Emotion* 18, no. 3 (2018): 439–52.

14: IF YOU BREAK IT, YOU OWN IT

1. Daniel Kahneman and Amos Tversky, "On the Psychology of Prediction," *Psychological Review* 80, no. 4 (1973): 237–51.
2. Amos Tversky and Daniel Kahneman, "Judgment under Uncertainty: Heuristics and Biases," *Science* 185, no. 4157 (September 27, 1974): 1124–31.
3. Janet Metcalfe, "Learning from Errors," *Annual Review of Psychology* 68 (January 2017): 465–89.
4. Melvyn R. W. Hamstra, Jan Willem Bolderdijk, and Janet L. Veldstra, "Everyday Risk Taking as a Function of Regulatory Focus," *Journal of Research in Personality* 45, no. 1 (February 2011): 134–37.
5. Greg McKeown, "To Build a Top Performing Team, Ask for 85% Effort," *Harvard Business Review*, June 8, 2023, https://hbr.org/2023/06/to-build-a-top-performing-team-ask-for-85-effort/.
6. Aaron T. Beck and Gary Emery, *Anxiety Disorders and Phobias: A Cognitive Perspective* (New York: Basic Books, 1985).

15: RUNNING MAN

1. Michiko Kakutuni, "It's True: Success Succeeds, and Advantages Can Help," *New York Times*, November 17, 2008, https://www.nytimes.com/2008/11/18/books/18kaku.html/.
2. Paul Marsden, "Mental Epidemics," *New Scientist*, May 6, 2000, https://www.newscientist.com/article/mg16622375-000-mental-epidemics/.
3. Jeremy Bentham, *An Introduction to the Principles of Morals and Legislation* (London, 1789; repr., Oxford: Clarendon Press, 1879), 1.
4. William James quoted in Andrew J. Elliot, "The Hierarchical Model of Approach-Avoidance Motivation," *Motivation and Emotion* 30, no. 2 (June 2006): 111.
5. Andrew J. Elliot, ed., *Handbook of Approach and Avoidance Motivation* (New York: Taylor & Francis, 2008), 10.
6. Andrew J. Elliot and Holly A. McGregor, "A 2 × 2 Achievement Goal Framework," *Journal of Personality and Social Psychology* 80, no. 3 (March 2001): 501–19.

16: HOW TO TALK ABOUT MISTAKES

1. Bernard Baruch, *Baruch: My Own Story* (New York: Henry Holt, 1957), 248.
2. Albert Ellis, *Reason and Emotion in Psychotherapy* (Secaucus, NJ: Carol Publishing Group, 1994).
3. Daniel Kahneman and Gary Klein, "Strategic Decisions: When Can You Trust Your Gut?," *McKinsey Quarterly*, March 1, 2010, https://www.mckinsey.com/capabilities/strategy-and-corporate-finance/our-insights/strategic-decisions-when-can-you-trust-your-gut/.
4. James W. Pennebaker, *Opening Up: The Healing Power of Expressing Emotions* (New York: Guilford Press, 1990).
5. Ellis, *Reason and Emotion in Psychotherapy.*
6. Kendra Cherry, "What Is a Schema in Psychology?," *Verywell Mind*, May 13, 2024, https://www.verywellmind.com/what-is-a-schema-2795873/.

17: HOW TO MAKE FEWER MISTAKES

1. Charles T. Munger, *Poor Charlie's Almanack: The Wit and Wisdom of Charles T. Munger* (Virginia Beach, VA: Donning, 2005), 54.
2. Groucho Marx quoted in Eve Starr, "Inside TV," *Greensboro Record*, November 3, 1954.
3. *Star Trek*, season 1, episode 10, "The Corbomite Maneuver," written by Jerry Sohl and Gene Roddenberry, directed by Joseph Sargent, aired November 10, 1966, on NBC; season 1, episode 16, "The Galileo Seven," written by Oliver Crawford and S. Bar-David, directed by Robert Gist, aired January 5, 1967, on NBC.
4. Antonio Damasio, *Descartes' Error: Emotion, Reason, and the Human Brain* (New York: G. P. Putnam's Sons, 1994).
5. Daniel Kahneman, *Thinking, Fast and Slow* (New York: Farrar, Straus and Giroux, 2011).
6. Jonathan Haidt, *The Happiness Hypothesis: Finding Modern Truth in Ancient Wisdom* (New York: Basic Books, 2006), 6.

7. Haidt, *The Happiness Hypothesis*, 6.
8. Marsha M. Linehan, *DBT Skills Training Manual* (New York: Guilford Press, 2015).
9. Anne-Laure Le Cunff, "Why Smart People Make Dumb Decisions," *Ness Labs*, December 14, 2023, https://newsletter.nesslabs.com/posts/ness-labs-why-smart-people-make-dumb-decisions/.
10. Patrick J. McGinnis, "Meet FOBO: The Evil Brother of FOMO That Can Ruin Your Life," Patrickmcginnis.com, https://patrickmcginnis.com/blog/meet-fobo-the-evil-brother-of-fomo-that-can-ruin-your-life/.
11. Beverly Engel, *The Power of Apology: Healing Steps to Transform All Your Relationships* (New York: John Wiley & Sons, 2001).
12. Gerd Gigerenzer, *Gut Feelings: The Intelligence of the Unconscious* (New York: Penguin Books, 2007).
13. Richard Wollheim, *F. H. Bradley* (Harmondsworth, UK: Penguin Books, 1959), 285.

About the Authors

Michael Lynton has spent his career in the media and entertainment business. His last full-time position was as the CEO of Sony Entertainment. He serves on the boards of the RAND Corporation and the Smithsonian. Lynton grew up in the Netherlands and received a BA from Harvard College and an MBA from Harvard Business School. He lives in New York City with his wife, Jamie Lynton, and their three children.

Joshua L. Steiner has had a varied career across government, finance, and the nonprofit sector. After serving as chief of staff at the US Department of the Treasury, he became a banker at Lazard before serving as an executive at Bloomberg LP and cofounding two investment firms. He grew up in Cambridge, Massachusetts, and attended Yale University, where he studied history and played lacrosse, before earning an MSt in modern history from Oxford. Steiner serves on the boards of Yale University, the International Rescue Committee, and the SNF Agora Institute at Johns Hopkins University. He lives in New York City with his wife, Antoinette Delruelle, and their three children.